THE HOUSE OF SATAN

THE BOOKS OF GEORGE JEAN NATHAN

The Theatre and Drama

THE CRITIC AND THE DRAMA*
THE POPULAR THEATRE
MATERIA CRITICA
MR. GEORGE JEAN NATHAN PRESENTS
COMEDIANS ALL**
ANOTHER BOOK ON THE THEATRE
THE THEATRE, THE DRAMA, THE GIRLS
THE HOUSE OF SATAN

Art and Life

THE WORLD IN FALSEFACE*

Philosophy

THE AUTOBIOGRAPHY OF AN ATTITUDE*
THE AMERICAN CREDO: A CONTRIBUTION TOWARD THE INTERPRE-
TATION OF THE NATIONAL MIND (*in collaboration with H. L.
Mencken*)

Satire

A BOOK WITHOUT A TITLE
BOTTOMS UP

Plays

HELIOGABALUS*** (*in collaboration with H. L. Mencken*)

Travel and Reminiscence

EUROPE AFTER 8:15* (*in collaboration with H. L. Mencken*)

In Collaborative Compilations

CIVILIZATION IN THE UNITED STATES, *by Thirty Americans*
ESSAYS BY PRESENT-DAY WRITERS, *by Raymond Woodbury Pence*
READINGS FROM "THE AMERICAN MERCURY," *by Grant C. Knight*
A PORTFOLIO OF AMERICAN EDITORS, *by Louis Evan Shipman*

Prefaces

THE MOON OF THE CARIBBEES AND OTHER PLAYS, *by Eugene O'Neill*
HOW'S YOUR SECOND ACT?, *by Arthur Hopkins*

* Also published in Great Britain
** Also published in Australia
*** Also published in Germany

THE HOUSE OF SATAN

GEORGE JEAN NATHAN

Mcmxxvi

New York   ALFRED · A · KNOPF   London

132591

BOX

CONTENTS

THE HOUSE OF SATAN

THE HOUSE OF SATAN

It has always been the mission of the theatre to reduce, in so far as it lay within its power, the manners and morals of the community. Obviously, I do not speak of the debased, uncivilized theatre, but of the theatre that is artistically on the highest and finest level. That for more than two thousand years men who have not taken the trouble to understand the theatre have sponsored the opposite point of view and have seen in the playhouse a medium for the uplifting of the human psyche and table manners through the operation known as dramatic catharsis, indicates only that it has taken the twentieth of the centuries to arrive at other astonishing discoveries in the world of high art than the radio, colored moving pictures and the Czech drama.

When I speak of the theatre as a corrupter of morals, it is of course as a synonym for drama. And when I speak of drama, I speak at the same time of most of the other arts, for the accomplishment, if perhaps not always the intention, of all art is the lowering of human virtue, in the commonly accepted sense of the word, and the conversion of men from metaphysical and emotional Methodism to metaphysical and emotional Paganism.   To believe the contrary, to believe that great art is an inspirer of virtue, is to be so vealy as to believe that "Tristan" makes its auditor feel like St. Francis of Assisi, that Byron and Swinburne conjure up Sunday-school memories, that the Venus of Cnidus makes one think of entering a monastery, and that "Lysistrata" is the most eloquent argument for continence ever written.   Only the fly-blown and ignorant, however, longer suffer any delusions about the purposes of art.   Such mammals hit upon a few obvious kindergarten exceptions to the general and seek to build their case upon them.   Unacquainted with nine-tenths of the world's best music, literature, painting, sculpture, poetry and drama, they imagine that all art has the same effect upon the human spirit as Chopin's E flat major nocturne or the slow movement of his B flat minor sonata, Botticelli's "Madonna and Child" and "Romeo and Juliet."   Yet if art were what these imbeciles imagine, it would have died from the cosmos hundreds of years ago.   It has been kept alive by man's unregenerate sinfulness alone.   Its greatest patron saints, the men who with power and gold and favor have encouraged and assisted its craftsmen, have almost without exception been the more dissolute kings and emperors, lechers and millionaire crooks, fleshpot fanciers and followers of Pan. And its greatest lovers and stoutest champions have ever been the men who most truly appreciated that behind its pretence of divine origin there curled a red and forked tail.

Art ennobles? Then tell me what, precisely, is the ennobling nature of—and how, precisely, one is made to feel *Corpsbruder* to the angels by— "Macbeth," Rembrandt's portrait of his sister, "Madame Bovary" or Richard Strauss' "Salomé." The simple truth, of course, is that, aside from a purely critical gratification, "Macbeth" exalts the cultured and intelligent man just about as much as a modern Edinburgh bathtub, that the chief thought that enters the man's mind when he gazes upon the Rembrandt portrait is that it would be charming to give the old boy's sister a hug, and that Flaubert and Strauss induce in the reader and auditor much less an overwhelming desire to lead a better and nobler life than a worse and more lamentably agreeable one. Such a contention, plainly enough, will be set down as a mere showy bout with paradox, since it is ever the custom of otherwise estimable folk to laugh off as unsound paradox any perfectly sound but more or less novel argument whose surface has upon it regrettable, but unavoidable, ripples of smart-aleckry. Yet that the thesis is deeply imbedded in fact may readily be determined by examining the lives and history of professional dramatic critics, for example, since the first and greatest of the craft saw the light of day at Stagira. If dramatic art is capable of ennobling the spirit, it is reasonable to suppose that men most constantly in audience with it should be among the blessed of God and that the dramatic critic, accordingly, should soon or late find himself upon a hyperphysical plane along with St. Peter, Emanuel Swedenborg and the Rev. Dr. S. Parkes Cadman. Yet it is well known that, with the exception of music critics, there has been and is no more spiritually disreputable body of men on earth than these very dramatic critics, beside whom an aisle full of Bobadils are paragons of virtue. If the influence of classic art is so powerful in the direction of the uplift, why have not those who have come most directly under that spell shown some of the good effects? However, glance at the leading subjects of the influence in question and see what happened to them! Scaliger, of the famous "Poetices Libri Septem," was one of the foulest liars of his time (he lied about everything from his mythical noble parentage to his conquests among women), was charged with heresy and found himself shunned by all the decent people of his day. Castelvetro, knowing that the authorities would get him for heresy, ran off like a frightened cur to Chiavenna and was later disgraced by excommunication. Sebillet, of the "Art Poétique," was a scurvy political crook; Cervantes was a jail-bird and in his later life was caught by the government in peculiar financial dealings and was kicked out of his job; Lope de Vega was banished from Spain for dirty libels, later raped the daughter of a Madrid government official and, entering a monastery in 1614, promptly brought obloquy upon the order by various sexual peccadilloes; and Gabriel Tellez's chief amusement lay in the "Cigarreles de Toledo," at some of which even Abe Lincoln would have blushed.

Coming to the Sir Philip Sidney of "A Defence of Poesie," we find an unmitigated snob and one whose questionable adventures among the fair sex are well known. Ben Jonson was sent to jail on three different occasions and had the killing of a man to his credit. Scudéry was guilty of unremitting personal dishonesty; among other noble acts, he based his hostile attitude toward Corneille entirely upon personal reasons and went far beyond the truth in calling the latter a thief. Chapelain was so drunk that Richelieu had a hard time getting him to rewrite his report on "Le Cid" so that it made clear reading. Racine was lazy, lived on

As for Victor Hugo, he was banished from France because of questionable political dealings, entered into double-dealing with both political parties upon his return after the upheaval of 1870, and was driven from the country again. Dumas, *fils,* was always in debt and led a dissolute life; Sarcey periodically grafted on the leading personages of the theatre of his time; Brunetière was an absinthe fiend; and Zola was twice sentenced to a year's imprisonment and the payment of a heavy fine. Coleridge took opium to forget the ugliness of the world and once went around getting money for subscriptions to a paper which failed and didn't pay it back. Hazlitt, after one round in the divorce courts, found that his second wife also couldn't stand him and his temper became so bad and his meanness so marked that he got into nasty quarrels with such of his best friends as Coleridge, Southey and Wordsworth. And, to come to a conclusion, Charles Lamb was actually driven crazy from application to the presumably exalting classics and, having got his sister Mary similarly to apply herself to them, also succeeded in driving the poor girl to a point of insanity where she lost all reason and killed her own mother. My own remaining infinitesimal share of manners and morals after something like twenty-five years spent under the influence of the art of drama keeps me from going into the question of the more modern critics, many of whom are still alive. I therefore simply wink meaningly, and bow myself politely out. As for music critics, I content myself with refering you to the police records.

If fine art has the power of spiritual exaltation in it, I should like to ask the greatest æsthetician living in the world today just what is the nature of the psychic uplift he gets from such things as Rembrandt's "Old Woman Cutting Her Fingernails," Boëthus' sculptures of the boy choking a goose and the little girl playing with dice, Fielding's "Tom Jones" and Zola's "La Terre," Brahms' variations on a theme by Haydn or Molière's "Le Bourgeois Gentilhomme." The truth is that the inspirational value of art has become a proverb, a phrase for promiscuous mouthing, a something taken for granted, and has been brought to apply to all art when in reality it applies only to a negligible fraction of art, and that fraction not always of the highest level. It may be true that such eminently estimable, if become obvious, works as the "Ave Maria" instil in the heart of man a feeling that was not there before and that such others as the crucifix of Spirito, the "Coronation of the Virgin" and the Rheims Cathedral accomplish a like end, but for every "Ave Maria" one finds no difficulty in naming a half dozen equally eminently estimable

11

compositions by the same Johannes that do nothing of the kind and that make one feel considerably less devout than thirsty. And if the crucifix of Michelangelo, or the painting of Raphael alluded to, or the ecclesiastical architecture of a forgotten genius of the Middle Ages induces in the spectator one kind of feeling, you may be sure that Michelangelo's great cartoon of the Battle of Cascina, or certain of Raphael's frescoes, or the secular architecture of a forgotten genius of an earlier age in the instance of the Porta Martis induces quite another and vastly more material kind.

It is, as I have hinted, not art in its fullest bloom that uplifts and nobilitates mortal man, but only art of a relatively mediocre quality. "Oedipus Rex," by no stretch of honest imagination, can conceivably have the slightest inspirational effect upon any even half-way intelligent emotionalism, yet "Old Heidelberg," a comparatively tenth-rate piece of work, can. The so-called dramatic catharsis of "King Lear" isn't one-twentieth so strong as that of, say, "Peter Pan." "Das Wohltemperirte Klavier," from 1 to 48 inclusive, can't gild or stimulate the heart and fancy and make them better and braver than they were before, where "Der Alte Dessauer," "Madelon" or "Home Sweet Home" conceivably may. For what is the effect of truly great art? The effect of truly great art, I persuade myself to

12

believe, is to induce in the beholder a sense of inferiority, a sense of the pettiness and futility of his own life, and, inducing these, to cause him to try to forget his triviality and despair in rash, impudent and deplorable actions, manners and thoughts which he would otherwise not engage. It stings him to the quick, challenges him, jeers at him. "Come on, worm!" it cries. "*Try* to look into Paradise!" The worm, humiliated but rambunctious, thereupon digs his toes into the ground, cocks back his head, strains the heavens with his eyes—and has his pocket picked.

INTELLIGENCE AND DRAMA

Although we live in the enlightened years of the Twentieth Century, the talk of intelligence in the theatre continues to go on. We hear still of "intelligent drama" on the one hand and plays that "insult the intelligence" on the other. The whole canon of dramatic criticism in the last thirty years, indeed, appears to rest somewhat snootily upon the premise that the virtue of drama is predicated upon this intelligence, and that, save drama possess it and, possessing it, gratify intelligence in turn, the aforesaid drama may be dismissed from serious consideration without further ado.

Just how this notion of the consanguinity of intelligence and drama first got bruited about, one has trouble in ascertaining, for if intelligence were the chief desideratum in drama and if all the plays written in the world today were chock-full of it from beginning to end, there wouldn't be a single theatre between here and the island of Amorgopula that could pay its rent next Saturday night. But, of course, everyone except most dramatic critics knows perfectly well that the last thing necessary and valuable to drama is intelligence, and so the theatre prospers today as it has never before prospered. Intelligence is no more relevantly a part of drama than it is of music, painting, sculpture, hooch-dancing, six-day bicycle racing or any other art or diversion; it is a tremendous handicap rather than a magnificent asset. The drama, as I have observed in the past, is not the place for intelligence but only for a deft and superficially deceptive counterfeit of intelligence. To speak disparagingly, therefore, of drama that insults the intelligence is to speak disparagingly of graphic art that insults the intelligence and to complain of, say, Veronese's "St. Anthony Preaching to the Fishes" that it is of absolutely no worth because any man who thought he could accomplish anything by addressing lake trout on the subject of Holy Writ was a damned fool.

All fine art, as a matter of fact, not only insults the intelligence; it deliberately spits in the eye of intelligence. The imperishable tragedies of Shakespeare ask us to believe in ghosts and witches; and the great drama of Ibsen asks us to believe that the world is savagely cruel to a woman who has violated the Seventh Commandment, that dishonesty must inevitably turn upon its practitioner and smite him with a blow from which he cannot recover, that a syphilitic is doomed to end his days

15

a lunatic, and that, symbolism or no symbolism, when amorous old gentlemen afflicted with vertigo fall off the tops of towers, the young folk standing down below hear a harp recital going on in the air. Mozart, in "Don Giovanni," asks us to believe that a woman who could express herself in the harmonic beauty of a *"Non ti fider, O misera"* might be thought insane; and Wagner asks us to believe, in "Lohengrin," that a dove can pull a boat, in "Tannhäuser," that if a man speaks of physical love in high terms all the women will promptly leave the room, and, in "Siegfried," that a sword can split an anvil in two and that birds can speak excellent German. Bellini, in the "Madonna, Child and Six Saints," asks us to believe that an angel views the spectacle of a naked man with a puritanical Methodist concern; Raphael, in the "Victory of Leo IV at Ostia," asks us to believe that soldiers are constantly mindful of the picturesqueness of their poses in the heat of battle; and Tintoretto asks us, in "Adam and Eve," to believe that Adam looked like Bernarr Macfadden. To speak of intelligent art, which is to say, to demand that overpowering beauty be coincidently rational, is to speak of an intelligent Grand Canyon or an intelligent Granada or Lombard Plain, and to demand that moonlight and the summer stars satisfy the philosophical

16

doctrines of Spinoza, William Lloyd Garrison and
Herbert Croly.

In drama, a forthright metaphysic spells certain
disaster. Nothing is so corruptive of drama as
hard logic. What the drama calls for is not mental intelligence, but only emotional intelligence.
No matter how poorly the characters of drama reason, the demands of drama are fully satisfied so
long as their emotions are, or at least seem to be,
reasonable. A great dramatic character may have
the mind of an alley-cat or a congressman, but so
long as his emotions are rational and logical, so
long as he feels convincingly, so long as he doesn't
become angry when someone hands him an excellent cigar or doesn't fall in love with a woman who
is too fat, he may continue to be a great dramatic
character. Macbeth is a simpleton, but his emotions are those of a great man, hence he is a great
dramatic character. And it is the same with most
of the great characters of drama. It is almost
impossible to imagine a fine play built around,
say, Kant or Hegel as a philosopher. The theatre
has no call for such heroes. Its heroes must think
with their hearts and feel with their minds.
(Bahr's "The Master," on a not important dramatic level, may in this regard yet be offered as
supplementary reading.) To build a play around
Kant or Hegel and hope to keep even the most in-

telligent theatrical audience in the world in its seats after nine o'clock, one would inevitably have to make up either Immanuel or Georg Wilhelm to look like John Barrymore, have him crawl under Fifi's bed when her husband unexpectedly came back from Detroit, and introduce a scene in the second act in which he eluded the Scotland Yard detectives by hiding in the cuckoo clock.

Fine drama, as a matter of fact, generally insults the intelligence, as the phrase goes, vastly more than gimcrack drama. "Hamlet" frequently impresses the logical mind as mere gorgeously beautiful drivel, where some such relatively fifteenth-rate piece of work as "They Knew What They Wanted" satisfies the rational sense more or less completely. Great art is as irrational as great music. It is mad with its own loveliness. Æschylus and Richard Strauss are beer-brothers under their skins: the "Eumenides" is as drunk with the dazzling beauty of æsthetic scapulimancy on the one hand as "Also Sprach Zarathustra" is on the other. If you are looking for sense, go to the plays of Channing Pollock and the songs of Irving Berlin.

And so we come to Shaw's dramatic gigolo, the M. Eugène Brieux. Brieux's chief fault as a dramatist is his intelligence, or, more accurately, his dervish-like belief that what he knows con-

stitutes intelligence and his passion for inculcating
it in his plays. Take the average Brieux play, cut
out the names of its leading characters, run the text
together, borrow an ice-water pitcher, and you have
a first-class lyceum bureau lecture for use at the
Town Hall. The flame of intelligent nonsense is
never—or, at least, very seldom—present in his
work, as it is present in the work of such greatly
more intelligent men as, for instance, his British
god-father. He seizes upon an available theme
for a good play and then proceeds painstakingly
to think it right out of the theatre. Where a competent and persuasive dramatist would take the
same theme and carefully drain from it every
vestige of dialectic wind and every trace of polemic
dulness, Brieux goes carefully about the business
of draining from it every vestige of vagrant beauty
and every trace of human charm and boils it down
to its elemental and vastly depressing syllogistic
bones. He seems to be of the theory that drama
is designed to prove something to the human head,
unaware completely that the highest aim of drama
is rather to prove something only to the human
heart. He burns with the fervor of a shyster lawyer; for all the world like a movie comedian he
is not content to be what he is—in his case, a writer
of plays—but must needs also be regarded by the
world beyond the theatre as a thinker. It is thus

that he goes about composing his plays with his eye ever set upon convincing by stark logic, where the eye of the real dramatist is ever set, to the contrary, upon convincing by beautifully embellished equivocation. For in the theatre we believe not so much what may be true as what may be merely plausible. The logic of heredity, let us say, as we get it in some such drama as Brieux's "L'Evasion" is never one-tenth so effective in the theatre as the romantic sophistry of heredity as we get it in a Rostand's "L'Aiglon."

There is no man so stupid, in point of fact, as the intelligent dramatist who carries his intelligence full-fledged over into his plays. His intelligence is of very great service to him before he proceeds to the actual writing of his plays, since it tells him what he should not write and since it further safeguards him from writing the kind of plays that men less intelligent than himself write; but when he sets himself to the actual business of writing his plays he must leave his intelligence off stage and permit it simply to criticize confidentially from time to time the charming holiday from sound intelligence that is giving a show out on the stage and restrain that holiday from becoming too objectionably rowdy. To this Polichinelle secret, such playwrights as Brieux are seldom privy, and as a result their plays generally disclose themselves to be

20

masses of platitudes, since by the time almost any philosophic idea finds its way into the theatre it is, by the intrinsic nature of the theatre, already a great-grandfather. These playwrights, however, constantly bemuse themselves with the theory that because they have thought of something for the first time, it is therefore of a revolutionary newness and must so impress others. And their plays, as a consequence, generally take on the aspect of so many rush telegrams, delivered by a breathless messenger-boy, which contain information that the recipient has read in day before yesterday's newspaper, and not been the least interested in. Once in his life, Brieux forgot himself and wrote an excellent comedy, "Les Hannetons." Once again, he partly forgot himself and came near writing a very good play, "Les Trois Filles de M. Dupont." But for most of the rest of his life he has been writing such things as "La Robe Rouge," "La Femme Seule" and "L'Avocat" which turn their stages into lecture platforms, Hyde Park soapboxes and street-corner cart-tails, and their auditors into somnambulists groping their way to the exits.

As for Shaw, his plays live in the theatre not because he is a thinker, as some idiots maintain, and not because he is a fellow of profound emotion, which no one is sufficiently idiotic to maintain, but, very simply, because he is a great humorist.

If there is a play that lives on in the theatre solely because of its thought, using the term in its commonly accepted sense, its name is beyond me. Thought, as I have said before, is no more essential to good drama than it is to roller-skating. The plays that endure are uniformly without such so-called thought; what they have, instead, is deep and honest emotional content. But, since Shaw's plays are generally as lacking in deep and honest emotion as so many undertakers, we must look elsewhere for their longevity and, looking, find it in their precious jocosity.

There are plays that are, however, as humorous as Shaw's and that still lack the measure of sustained life enjoyed by the works of the Adelphi Terrace flat-dweller. But these other plays have not the Shaw trick of making humor comparatively ageless by founding it upon ageless institutions, philosophies and events. You can write the funniest play in the world about a Tennessee monkey trial, or the Ku Klux Klan, or Prohibition, or Barney Baruch's visits to the White House, and it will go the way of all things as soon as its immediate day is done. Because of the transitory nature of the situations and events upon which it is based, its humor will get arterio-sclerosis years before even such lower humors as are based on the more permanent squirting dill pickle and porous

Swiss cheese. Humor, to live, must be extracted from eternally humorous characters and phenomena, as Aristophanes, Shakespeare, Molière and Sheridan extracted it and as Shaw more lately has extracted it.

Shaw's device is not, as has been said, to take the common serious beliefs of men and wittily laugh them out of men's belief. His device is rather to take these common serious beliefs of men and laugh them back into men's wit. A man who sees a Shaw play doesn't come away from it with his belief in this or that taken from him; he comes away from it with his belief purged of its dulness and of its everyday lack-lustre and clothed instead in stimulating spangles and rhinestones. He doesn't cease believing; he simply joins his belief with a tonic and healthy laughter. Shaw sells men laughter against their wish, and makes them like it. In this lies his really great showmanship. He is the only dramatist of modern times who knows the trick of simultaneously insulting them and patting them on the back, and patting them so jovially that they are not conscious of the detraction. He carefully and shrewdly keeps them from thinking by assuring them in a loud voice that he will do their thinking for them and by then cleverly not thinking at all but merely announcing in an even louder voice that what they have been thinking is nonsense. To keep the more stubbornly minded persons in his audiences from seeing through his stratagem, he then further ingeniously sets about distracting them with low comedy which has very little to do with the matter immediately in hand, but which is so loaded with good, loud belly-laughs that Kant, Hegel, Huxley, Schopenhauer and Spencer themselves would gladly forget all about sound sense, open their top pant-buttons, and let go.

In Shaw, we have perhaps the most proficient sure-fire playwright of our time, the only difference between him and his other sure-fire contemporaries being that, where the latter direct their sure-fire at the theatre of their day and hour, Shaw diffuses his, as with a shot-gun instead of a rifle, over a considerably broader period. In his determination to make his plays sure-fire, the affable Bernard doesn't overlook a single fetch and doesn't hesitate to stoop to the cabbaging of the lowest hokum out of the lowest burlesque show. Beside him, Mr. Winchell Smith is in this respect an ethereal artist, and Mr. George Cohan a Dante. As I have shown in the past, he takes the low-comedy horse out of Lew Fields' "About Town" and turns it into the low-comedy lion of "Androcles"; he takes the comically drunk Leon Errol and presents him as the comically drunk Patiomkin; he steals the

frequent falls of Bozo Snyder upon his caudal
vertebræ and gives them to his Edstaston; he
sprinkles his plays with all the "hells" and
"damns" of Hal Reid and Harry Clay Blaney; he
resorts to the repeated mispronunciation of a
character's name (as in the instance of Szczepanow-
ska in "Misalliance"), an old comic standby of the
music halls; he goes in for box-office smut (*vide*
"Misalliance"), for cheap box-office sensationalism
(*vide* the use of "bloody" in "Pygmalion"), for
the sure-fire glass-smashing business, for Sam
Bernard's comic word reiteration (*vide* "Can-
dida"), for the mimicry of one character by
another (*vide* "You Never Can Tell")—always
bait for the gallery laughter—, for loud box-office
sex (*vide* "Mrs. Warren"), and for the 10–20–30
hokum of the entrance of the United States marines
in the nick of time to save the hero (*vide* "Brass-
bound"). In short, he stoops to conquer the hooli-
gans even while he is drawing himself up to his
full height to look the more cultivated theatregoer
in the eye and tell him to go to.

As I have hinted, however, he contrives to make
this ancient and largely irrelevant hokum seem
other than it actually is by imbedding it in a very
mild and obvious but exceptionally jocular philosophy. Thus, when one of his characters kicks
another in the rear, he doesn't then sit back con-

tentedly and consider the resulting laugh a sufficient reward for his efforts. He accompanies the kick in the character's rear with an equally low-comedy kick in the rear of some generally accepted belief, and the laugh he gets is twice as great. The drama of Shaw, roughly speaking, indeed, consists for the most part in a dramatization of the *contra mundum* attitude placed in the mouths of characters who, for all their looks and dress, are really Clark and McCullough under their skins. He doesn't seek to convince his audiences by straight line rushes; he makes his scores by grotesque forward passes, by hiding the ball under his sweater, by running backward and so deceiving his opponents, and by pretending that he has been knocked out and then, when no one is looking, jumping up and zigzagging safely to his destination. And his plays live, where the plays of others die, because he is sagacious enough to dramatize the hokum of yesterday and to-day in terms of the hokum of tomorrow. And, further, because he is shrewd enough to appreciate that the way to make plays live longer than their accustomed span in the theatre is to conceive of them as dramatic literature first and theatrical plays secondly.

L'HOMME POUDRÉ

§ 1

The actor is, of all mortals, perhaps the most generally ridiculed. He is the butt of all manner of folk, including his fellow actors. From time immemorial he has been the seat of humor whereon the slapstick of the world has enjoyed a continuous explosion. The mocked at of men, he has been driven to seek unction to his vanity and ointment to his *amour propre* in the adulation and respect of male milliners, flappers and servant girls. He has been ever the target of drawing-room epigram and bar-room jest; he has been ever the tin can on his own tail. Why?

The reasons usually assigned for this attitude toward the actor do not entirely convince me. There have been, and there are still, actors of high talent and men of personal and professional dignity. Yet these, who have been worthy of respect, have suffered from the stigma that attaches to their craft scarcely less than the rank and file of the bounders. The springs of this stigma have often been inquired into. It has been argued, for example, by Lemaître—and after him, by the brother of an actor, Max Beerbohm—that the prejudice against actors is less strong as regards women, and reasonably, in that when women play they compromise their dignity much less than men do, since they are, in life, actors naturally, and since gaudy clothes, gaudy manners and gaudy cosmetics are part and parcel of the charade that is their daily game. Although this is true, although the stage is, of all places, the place for women, I can't see that a man compromises his dignity in becoming an actor much more than a man compromises his dignity by becoming a poet and giving public readings of his own verses. The poet who thus postures himself before halls full of sentimental maiden ladies is a not less ridiculous spectacle than the actor, yet no stigma attaches to him in the minds of his fellow men, although, true enough, they may permit themselves an occasional esoteric snicker at his expense. So far, too, as the actor's painting his face goes, one of the leading local orchestra conductors, two of the foremost French dramatists and one of the best Spanish dramatists, one of the leading figures in Italian letters and one of the most conspicuous of modern European painters are each and all notoriously guilty of the same thing, and without the actor's legitimate reason, and yet none of these is vouchsafed the derisory hoot that greets the mummer. It is said, further, that one cannot have respect for a man who always has to go to his work up an alley, but if the actor's work is always up an alley so is the work of many sculptors and paint-ers. The actor, it is continued, is an absurd fel-low, a professional lady's man, a professional, rooster, a popinjay. Well, so is one of England's greatest novelists, so is one of England's best criti-cal intelligences and essayists, so is one of Italy's best poets, so is one of France's most skilful dram-atists—and yet these are the admired and respected of cultivated men.

The actor, so runs the objection to him, is a para-site: he lives on the labor of an artist, his dramatist. But if the actor is a parasite in this respect, so, in a measure, is the dramatic critic, yet no one would think of an actor, even the best, in the same breath with, say, Shaw, even on his off-days on the *Saturday Review*. The actor, pursues the prose-cution, is an idiot who thrives on the applause of other idiots. True, but the idiots who applaud him are not looked down upon by their fellow men as the latter look down upon the actor. The Poli vaudeville actor who climbs in through the window, finds his wife in the embrace of the piano-mover and demands of Gus, the orchestra leader, what he would do in such a case, being informed in turn that Gus would give the piano-mover a box of good cigars, is an actor, and is ever regarded as an actor. The man who loudly applauds him from the right-hand stage box may be a President of the United States named Woodrow Wilson, who is regarded as a great statesman and savior of democracy.

These are each and all poor arguments. They do not account for the disesteem in which the actor as actor is held. But if the actor is generally disesteemed, as he is, and the usually assigned reasons do not hold water, what are the reasons? The reasons, it seems to me, are obvious. In the first place, the actor brings obloquy down upon his own head by being privately more or less ashamed of his job. The one ambition of an actor, above every other ambition, is not to be like an actor. The highest compliment one can pay a mummer is to tell him that he doesn't look like an actor, or act like one. If one were to tell the same thing to a musician or a painter, to wit, that he didn't look or act like what he pretended to be or actually was, he would feel that he had been insulted. But it is a rare actor who isn't flattered if he be told that he looks and acts like a good, all-around, everyday, 100 per cent butter and egg man. To the end that he may not seem an actor, the actor will go to the greatest extremes. He will lay aside his bizarre suit, white spats, yellow gloves and gardenia and dress himself with such sedulous simplicity that, in leaning backward, his get-up touches his toes. He will studiously avoid talking of the theatre; he will avoid the gathering places of actors; he will shun actors as companions. Secondly, the actor makes a laughing-stock of himself by posturing an intelligence that he hasn't got, and that, even if he had it, would be as valuable to his craft as a knowledge of the bagpipe is to a man with lockjaw. For one actor who confines himself to the subject of acting, regarding which he may be assumed to have some opinions, usually worthless, you will find a dozen who, when interviewed, seize the occasion to discuss subjects about which they knew absolutely nothing and who rely faithfully on the ignorance of the interviewer to get them safely over the tough spots. Ask the average actor what he thinks about this or that concerned with acting and he will exhaust his profundity in a couple of minutes, and breathe a sigh of relief when he is through. But ask him what he thinks of the relative values of the art of Domenico Alaleona and Rachmaninoff, the multiplicity of prose meanings in Browning's "Sordello," the communistic philosophy of the Karmathians and the first $3\frac{1}{2}$'s of the Spuyten Duyvil and Port Morris Railroad and he will talk

31

himself through a box of throat lozenges. Ask a
novelist, or a composer, or a sculptor, or an
architect—or, for that matter, a lime and cement
dealer—to talk and, once he gets through with the
inevitable preliminary disquisition on ethyl alcohol, he will talk about the thing that he knows
about, that is closest to his heart and that interests
him most, which is to say, his trade. Ask an actor
to talk and, once he gets through with the inevitable
preliminary disquisition on women, he will talk
about everything save that which he knows. In
every generation, there are a few actors who adorn
their profession by being and remaining actors.
In every generation, there are a thousand more
who bring it into disrepute by trying to be what
they are not. The place of the actor is the stage;
when he seeks to constitute himself a critic of life
and art he is as absurd as Georg Brandes would
be in the rôle of Charley's Aunt.

There was a gipsy day when the actor was proud
of being an actor and when, accordingly, his fellow
men respected him for his pride, as men always
respect lack of affectation and honesty in others,
however humble and grotesque their lot. Then,
as Moore has said, a great and drastic change
came; the mummer grew ashamed of his hose and
longed for a silk hat, a villa, and, above all, a visit
from the parson. He began to patronize not

too scrupulous merchants of genealogy in order to learn of possible aristocratic connections, of his possible descent from William the Conqueror or Theobald of Blois, and of his right to have his letter paper engraved with a crest including at least two bags of spears and three lions. He began to jockey for invitations to lecture at the universities, to attend Chamber of Commerce banquets, and to join so-called exclusive supper clubs. He hired himself private cars, like Charlie Schwab, and went in heavily for rare first editions, like Mr. Guggenheim. He went in, in short, for almost everything but the art of acting. For a study of diction, he substituted the joys of a pink and green Rolls-Royce; for a study of gesture, he substituted lunch at the Colony restaurant; for a study of drama, he substituted a place on one of S. Stanwood Menken's committees to make the world safe for Sinclair, Doheny and Jesus. And slowly his profession showed the results of his monkeyshines. Slowly it dropped and dropped until today we are entertained by the spectacle of a horde of incompetents who have no more claim to the title of actor than a Bowery bum has to the title of archduke. For one actor who knows his craft, we have a score who know little more about acting than a cannibal knows about Listerine. For one actor who is a credit to his calling, we have fifty who look on that

calling much in the way that a street-walker looks
on a drunken gob.

And yet, though the actor runs away from being
an actor, though he is ashamed of the work in
which he is engaged and upon which he depends
for his livelihood and his place in the sun, he
makes himself further ridiculous by the paradox
of rushing noisily to the rescue of his fellow actor
when the latter calls to him as a actor. If a dozen
actors, so abysmally bad that they have caused a
play to close three nights after it has opened, have
ten dollars apiece still coming to them from the
manager, who has had to go out and pawn his hat
in order to pay off the charwoman, the dozen best
actors in the country will promptly cast off all dignity and honor to their art by hurrying around to
the manager, either personally or through representatives, and threatening him that they will send
him to Coventry unless he promptly goes out once
again and pawns his pants in order to pay their colleagues what is due them. This unionization of
actors has been the last and most ludicrous straw
upon the camel's back. If some poor, forgotten
wop house-painter had made a botch of painting
the water-closet in Lorenzo de' Medici's palace
and had been packed off by Lorenzo's major-domo
without pay and if thereupon Michelangelo, Leon-
ardo da Vinci, Perugino, Lorenzo di Credi, Veroc-

chio, Correggio, Raphael, Botticelli, Filippo Lippi, Pollajuolo, Bellini, Titian, Carpaccio, Tintoretto, Veronese, Piero della Francesca, Gozzoli, Palma Vecchio, Signorelli, Lazzaro Vasari, Giorgione, Pinturicchio, Mantegna, Ferrari and Bordone had promptly sent a committee around to the palace and instructed Lorenzo that if he didn't settle with their brother at once he would forever be outlawed, a homeric horselaugh would have descended down the ages. Yet our leading actor-artists (as they like to call themselves) ask us to take them seriously as artists when a poor, deluded fellow goes down into his sock to put on a measle of his own composition called "Flesh," hires a bunch of the most outrageous, but inexpensive, hams in Christendom to play it for him, and is then told by the union representatives of these leading actor-artists that he cannot ring up his curtain unless the "rights" of the outrageous and unspeakable hams who are about to outrage the public in an unspeakably outrageous play are duly safeguarded by him. No artist worth the name can conceivably have any interest in the affairs of a hack, whether artistically, commercially, psychically or in any other way. If he is concerned with a hack's affairs and well-being, he is no artist, but simply a brother Elk. The artist not only does not care whether the hack starves to death; he hopes that he will starve to death, and the sooner the better. Trades unions are not for artists. They are, evidently, only for garment workers, hod carriers, plumbers and actors.

It is, as I have said, the misfortune of the actor who dignifies his craft to be compelled to share the derisions that have come to be attached to it through the imbecilities and pollutions practised by those who use it as a parade ground for their ignorance, their insolence, their vainglory and their imitation Fifth Avenue clothes. There is only one union that actors should form, and that is a union of competence. But such a union, one fears, would have very few members.

§ 2

The present American scene discloses the usual number of actresses who devote themselves to studying French, learning the piano, taking fencing lessons, visiting art galleries, studying Delsarte and keeping away from Broadway supper clubs in the fond belief that by doing so they are improving their positions in their art. These misguided young women are the source of much mirth. What they gain from their nonsensically irrelevant didoes is not the knowledge of how to act on the stage but merely the knowledge of how to act in a drawing-room. They do not wish to be actresses so much as they wish to be ladies. And being a lady has nothing to do with acting. Ellen Terry didn't learn how to act by lunching only at the Ritz and never under any circumstances being seen at Lüchow's, nor did Bernhardt learn her art by hanging around the Louvre and spending her nights reading the poetry of Verlaine.

§ 3

Although the statement seems superficially to wear cap and bells, it remains that the exceptionally good actor or actress, cast for a rôle in a drama dealing with modern life, frequently by the very fact of his or her artistic virtuosity diminishes the verisimilitude implicit in the rôle. The circumstance that the logic of this is all wrong doesn't alter the circumstance that, in actual operation, the thing is a demonstrated fact. While it should be logical that a highly gifted performer should be able, by the artifice of his craft, to achieve the semblance and effect of naturalness and humanness demanded by the rôle he plays, it occasionally happens that his technical proficiency smothers to a degree that naturalness and humanness and substitutes for the human and natural character a discernibly experienced and excellent but more or less highly mechanized actor. Such an actor as the late Lucien Guitry and such an actress as, say, the living Mrs. Fiske were and are respectively professors of every technical phase of their calling, yet neither ever played a character in modern drama that didn't seem less a child of God than a child of the green-room. A too highly developed technic frequently runs away from nature in this wise. There is no better technical dramatist in America than Augustus Thomas, and none whose plays have less of life and earth in them. There is no better actress in America, in certain limited modern rôles, than, say, Miss Chrystal Herne, and there is none who gives one less sense and feeling of character actuality. It is all very well to say that if an actor or actress, however ostensibly gifted, fails to give this sense of reality, that actor or actress is not so gifted as one thinks. But it is often the very performer about whose gifts there isn't a dissenting critical voice who fails most signally in this regard. The reasons I have set down for the failure may not be the correct reasons, but the failure is still a disconcerting truth.

§ 4

It is the belief and common asseveration of the actor that wherever three or more actors get

38

together, there you have a theatre. The more cynical of us know, of course, that wherever three or more actors get together, there you have three or more pairs of yellow gloves, some good telephone numbers, and a loud denunciation of all managers, playwrights and other actors, but no more of a theatre than that portion of it that is represented on the three or more passes for two in the gathering's pockets. It is perfectly true that without actors the theatre would be in the position of a beer-wagon without horses, but it is also perfectly true that, without professional management, the theatre is in the position of a beer-wagon with the horses but without a driver.

§ 5

A student of theatrical critical phenomena of long standing, I am brought to the conclusion that there is one type of play, however bad, that invariably gets good notices from the gentlemen of the press. I allude to the play in which, at the end of the second act, the star actor or actress lets loose a wild eye-rolling, arm-waving, bosom-shaking slice of histrionic hell. If there is present on the records a play that has postured such an instance of earthquake mummerismus and that has not, because of it, been hailed as a thing of high merit, it

39

must date back to the time when roses were last passed across the footlights to the Cherry Sisters.

For some reason which evades me, our reviewers are regularly in the habit of confusing the acting performances in such plays with the plays themselves. The acting nonsense never fails to impress them deeply, and they carry over that impression into their appraisals of the dramatic manuscripts. It is thus that we periodically read of the great virtues of actors and actresses whose proficiency in their art is actually little more than the ability to imitate a person in the throes of peripheral epilepsy, and of the great virtues of plays that have nothing more to recommend them than the opportunity they afford the aforesaid actors and actresses to flabbergast and hornswoggle the critical suckers. And it is thus, further, that hardly a season passes without some such flapdoodle as "The Witching Hour," "The City" or "Children of the Moon" working the boys up to a pretty pitch of excitement. The acting performances which galvanize the reviewers customarily take the following form. The star Westphalian, along toward the conclusion of the middle act, comes onto the darkened stage shouting that some one or something that he cannot see is following him—faces, faces, faces—shapes, shapes, shapes—, whereupon he curls up his shoulders as if it were raining and the water were trickling down his undershirt. He wriggles, hisses, and works his eyeballs right and left. His face twists itself now in the manner of Gaspard in "The Chimes of Normandy," now in the manner of Thomas Shea in "Dr. Jekyll and Mr. Hyde," now in the manner of Houdini getting out of a pair of handcuffs, now in the manner of Lew Dockstader anticipating a boot in the behind. He makes a fist and shakes his body a couple of times after the fashion of a moist Spitz dog. He screams and permits his hands to tremble like La Belle Fatima's Little Mary. He gurgles, chokes and strangles over imaginary bootleg vodka. He lets out a few hoarse yelps and dejects himself upon the floor, where he writhes for a moment like Ruth St. Denis and then lies still. And the boobs out front proceed to a thunderous pounding of palms and bombardment of bravos.

§ 6

The American actor can play the rôle of an Englishman, a German, an Italian, a Russian, a Greek or a Zulu, but it seems that one thing he cannot play is the rôle of a Frenchman. I have seen hundreds of American actors try to play Frenchmen, yet thus far I haven't been successful in laying eyes on one who got much further into

his rôle than pronouncing Montmartre correctly
and wearing a top hat in the mornings. Those
American actors who, appearing in French drama
or farce, have been most highly praised for the
accuracy with which they have interpreted French
characters are simply those who have interpreted
the French characters not as French characters but
rather as the French characters are customarily regarded by American eyes. The American theatregoer has definite and fixed ideas as to the way a
Frenchman looks and comports himself, and the
American actor has exactly the same ideas. To
the American theatregoer and actor, all Frenchmen, from hack-drivers to members of the Acad-
emy, are cut from the same cloth. To them, the
Frenchman is not conceivable as a diversified human being susceptible of as many interpretations
as, say, an Englishman, but only as a fixed pattern,
and that pattern something of a freak. This point
of view has gone so far and has become so fixed
that when French actors come to America to interpret French characters in French plays, they invariably fail. The American, his mind made up as
to French characters through long association with
their American interpreters, actually feels that the
French interpreters are faulty. And, as a consequence, the American generally comes to the conclusion that the French actor is a bad actor. Lucien

Guitry, the best French actor of his time, is dead;
but if he had come to America in French drama, I
feel as certain that he would have failed as I feel
certain that his talented son would fail were he to
present himself to local audiences. Some of the
critics would praise him, of course, but the audiences would not cotton to him. They would not
understand his Frenchmen and they would not believe them. The characters in his plays they would
understand and believe, but his interpretations of
those characters would fail to make much of an
impression upon them. It would be the old case
of the giraffe. The American, when it comes to
giraffes—which is to say authentic French char-
acterizations—has spent his entire life looking at
mocking-birds.

It is not, however, that the American actor
doesn't occasionally try to work himself into the
soul and fibre of the French character he is called
upon to interpret. It is, rather, that, try as he will,
he is unable, for one reason or another, to penetrate
it and, penetrating it, expound it convincingly in
its various detail. The trick of dialect—I am
speaking, plainly enough, of translated or adapted
plays—he now and then masters; the Frenchman's
dress he now and then similarly duplicates; the
Frenchman's gestures and carriage he also now
and then manages to get in hand. But he simply

cannot get in hand the sense and feel of the Frenchman. What we customarily engage, accordingly,
is a French character more or less accurate in the
matter of externals, but otherwise little more Gallic
than the Paris *Herald* or the Ritz bar. It has been
said that the reason for this is the ineradicable
difference between the Anglo-Saxon and the Frenchman, a difference that makes impossible even an
Anglo-Saxon mummer's interpretation of a Frenchman. But the argument does not convince me.
Surely, there is an equal difference between, let
us say, the Anglo-Saxon and the Spaniard, yet
even so poor an American actor as Robert Edeson
has, in the Maugham play called "The Noble
Spaniard," done excellently by the rôle. On the
other hand, were I to be threatened with a year in
the calabozo if I didn't name an American actor
who had performed the rôle of a Frenchman with
moderate accuracy, I fear that I should have at once
to put in an order with my tailor for black and
white striped mufti.

But if the reasons usually assigned for the complete inability of American actors to play French
characters are wrong, what are the reasons? I
answer the question with the utmost ease: I don't
know. I have thought up eight or nine reasons
that have a superficial ring of truth to them, but
none of them, duly meditated, holds water. I con-

clude, indeed, that it may not be the fault of the American actor at all. The burden perhaps lies with the French dramatist. The latter, particularly if he be a writer of comedy or farce, has his characters ready-made to his hand in the persons of French actors, who are 100 per cent Frenchmen and typical of the French as a nation from the crowns of their heads to the tips of their spats. The French actor, in heart, in processes of mind and in general deportment, is the symbol of all Frenchmen, or at least of all Frenchmen who are material for the pen of a dramatic writer. He is an exaggerated symbol, true enough, but the stage is the home of exaggeration. Hence, the French dramatist—with obvious exceptions—may almost be said to have his characters written for him by whoever is the Chamberlain Brown of Paris. Such a playwright as Sacha Guitry, indeed, doesn't go to the trouble of creating characters at all; he simply and regularly writes himself and then plays it. And to ask an American subsequently to play the rôle, which is less a rôle than it is Sacha Guitry himself, is to ask not one actor to play another actor's rôle but to ask one man to *be* another man. Nor have I, for purposes of argument, hit on an unduly exaggerated case. We hear much in America of so-called type actors. In France, it is not a case of type actors but of type men. The French dramatist doesn't pick out an *actor* who is the type for a particular rôle; he picks out the *man* among the actors who *is* the rôle. Cataloguing is a sin for which I have received many a brick, so I shall refrain from persuading you in this direction with a lengthy list of names and dates. Let it therefore suffice to suggest the evidence merely by citing the instances of the casting of Edgar Becman during the heyday of the beauteous Lantelme, of Raymond Bernard cast by his father, Tristan, for the rôle of Bernhardt's *jeune premier,* of the casting by Bataille of the MM. Roger Vincent and Pierre Magnier in his "Vierge Folle," and of the original casting of Desjardins for the leading rôle in the light love symphony called "Petite Hollande." Now, obviously enough, when such rôles or rôles of a kind are imported by American producers and American actors bidden to interpret them, the latter must find themselves in sore straits. It is logical enough to request an American actor to play a rôle written for a French actor—though, as I have said, the request is factually ridiculous—but it is hardly logical to ask him to play a rôle written around and for a definite and peculiar Frenchman who happens to be an actor. If it be reasonable to ask him to do any such thing, then it is equally reasonable to ask and expect Firmin Gemièr to be a wow in "Forty-five Minutes From Broadway."

46

HOUSEBROKEN DRAMA

Whenever a critic, native or foreign, wishes to take a crack at American drama, he adjusts the monocle of the punctilio to his eye, squints through it in the manner of some unimpeachable *arbiter elegantiarum* and delivers himself—in a voice indicative of outraged gentility—of a treatise on bad manners. It would seem that the American drama, unlike that indigenous to other countries, is entirely ignorant of *bienséance* and etiquette and that when a playwright dares to bring it off the streets into a drawing-room it disconcertingly conducts itself very like a mutt dog. The American drama, we are told, may know how to comport itself in a police court, a Harlem flat or a waterfront dive, but the moment it aspires to an environment of somewhat nicer aspect it, like the mutt, shows clearly its inferior breeding and unaccustomedness to the dictates and usages of polite society and parlor rugs.

This attitude, I have the honor to believe, is for the most part buncombe. While it is unquestionably true that the American drama is a vulgar drama and one wherein bad manners are paraded proudly and gaudily before the city and out-of-town buyers like so many procurable mannequins, and while it is further equally true that the drama of certain other countries appears superficially to have a suavity and polish that the American drama lacks, it still seems to me that, in the broadest sense, the American drama is essentially no more burdened with bad manners than the English, French or German. Every now and again, of course, we get American confections in which, as in Miss Jane Cowl's "Daybreak," the male guests in a town house come down to breakfast in white flannels and carrying tennis rackets, in which, as in "Eve's Leaves," gentlemen make formal calls at half past eight in the morning, or in which, as in Mr. Shipman's "Cheaper to Marry," male dinner guests pass among the ladies tonily flicking their trousers' sides with gloves and their boots with walking sticks, but one can no more fairly appraise American drama by such occasional lapses and trivialities than one can appraise, say, Tintoretto's "Miracle of the Slave" by its fly-specks. The American drama is just as often deliberately as it is unconsciously loutish. The notion that Booth Tarkington and Harry Leon Wilson didn't knowingly load their "Man From Home" with bad manners, appreciating the box-office value of the latter, is just as untenable as the notion that the authors of "Dancing Mothers" intentionally made their butler suggest a Bronx cocktail to a lady visitor and caused their hero to spend the night at a fashionable New York club that doesn't happen to have any sleeping quarters. If we have a body of playwrights to whom good manners mean chiefly and consist chiefly in nonchalant and very airy allusions to polo, the Ritz hotel and other such *haut ton* delicatessen, the said allusions being customarily placed in the mouths of characters who wear dinner jackets with loop fasteners and who bump champagne glasses with the ladies, if, as I say, we have a corps of such absurd fellows, we have also a body whose work, while it may not be much in the way of drama, is certainly as circumspect in the matter of manners as that of any foreign national group. And what is more, the group in America is quite as large in point of numbers as any of the overseas groups. The American drama, taking it as a whole, is at this moment no more vulgar than that of England, and it is less vulgar, by long odds, than that of France or Germany.

All the arguments over the vulgarity of the American drama are either ridiculous or empty, or both. Drama, as a matter of fact, lies in bad manners. If anyone can point out to me a single one of the undisputed masterpieces of drama that

49

isn't as full of bad manners as a Pittsburgh stogie
is of burlap, I shall reward him with pearls and
rubies beyond price. Good manners produce
agreeable but trivial comedies, vehicles for actor-
manager tailors' dummies and vintage comediénnes
with lifted faces; bad manners produce the
"Lysistratas," the "Hamlets" and the "Cæsar and
Cleopatras." It is next to impossible, indeed, to
imagine a thoroughly interesting and meritorious
play in which there would be no deviation from the
punctilio. In a smashing of the punctilio lies the
conflict essential to drama. In every good play
there must obviously be a villain of one form or
another. That villain may be a sinister Italian
with waxed moustaches or perhaps merely an un-
popular bit of philosophy. But whatever he or it
is, you will generally find that the symbol is one of
bad manners, or at least what the public holds to
be bad manners.

Good manners, in the sound as opposed to the
superficial sense of the phrase, have seldom made
a dollar at the box-office, either in America or in
any other country. The kings and queens and the
dukes and duchesses of Shakespeare, the lacey
beaux and furbelowed ladies of Congreve, the
bachelor elegantos of the Edwardian stage and
the over-butlered puppets of Twentieth Century
drawing-room comedy have the most of them re-

vealed a bit of pig-sty mud on the soles of their otherwise immaculate boots. The bearing has been regal, the bow lordly, the cigarette-holder fourteen inches long, but the mind has eaten with its knife. The trick of effective polite drama, indeed, is to make your characters act good manners and think bad ones. That was the trick of the Restoration dramatists; that was the trick borrowed by Wilde; that is the trick today of the best of the Europeans. But as the mob always estimates manners in terms of outward show, the essentially vulgar drama has been praised for its adherence to the punctilio and the essentially well-mannered drama condemned for its vulgarity.

Our colonials, the English—theatrically speaking—have been leading propagandists against the vulgarity of the American drama. So shrewdly have they gone about their business that they have converted all the American critics to their point of view. Yet even a fugitive study of English drama in the last forty years or so makes immediately obvious the fact that the English drama is, if anything, actually and infinitely the more vulgar of the two. In the matter of manners—and I dare use the word even in its popular sense—there is no American playwright, including the M. Samuel Shipman himself, who is one-half so ill-mannered as Shaw, for example. Or take Pinero, who is regularly held up as a criterion of dramatic good manners. Take a close look at Pinero and you will find that he is every bit as vulgar as the English and their local apes accuse George M. Cohan of being. Mr. Cohan has, true enough, not been averse to having his heroes take running slides across ball-room floors, bring up against their hostesses and clap them a whack upon their décolleté backs, but if Mr. Cohan has ever written a play as consistently and unremittingly vulgar as Pinero has in the instance of "Tanqueray," wherein, in the very first ten minutes, the dinner guests comment on the quality of the food, wherein the hero deprecates the woman he is to marry, wherein the host turns his back upon his guests and, oblivious of their presence, proceeds to get off his day's correspondence, wherein his guests thereupon proceed to *sotto voce* innuendos about his wife-to-be, wherein the butler enters the dining-room and loudly announces a guest who has arrived for dinner after dinner is over, wherein the host sourly berates the latecomer for his tardiness, wherein a gentleman describes the wife of a friend as a common prostitute and is thereupon vouchsafed a bravo by another friend of the same friend, and wherein a guest, the moment his host leaves the room, alludes to the latter's dead wife as a sexless iceberg and to his daughter as an insensible little brat—if, to re-

52

peat, Mr. Cohan has ever written such a play, its title is lost to me. Nor do I single out "Tanqueray" especially. Pinero's napkin has been tucked under his chin in any number of his other works. And so have the napkins of Jones, Chambers, Carton, Grundy and most of the rest of them. Today, Maugham, Bennett, Lonsdale, Turner and the rest of the clever Englishmen wisely revel in bad manners, while our American playwrights idiotically strain themselves to keep close to the genteel coast of decorum. Good manners, the English playwright knows—even if he does not admit it when an American playwright is present—, are things for dramatic critics to expatiate on; bad manners are things for good dramatists to fashion interesting dramatic characters on.

Aside from the petty question of fashionable etiquette with its rules and regulations for the stenciling of human beings, we hear also and constantly of the question of thematic etiquette. The American drama, we are told, is as vulgar in its themes as it is in its character manipulation of them. If we were to believe the English critics and their American lap-dogs, we would be persuaded that the American drama consists entirely of spectacles wherein bounders triumph over gentlemen, wherein pants-makers are eulogized over artists and wherein the happiest of all endings is

one in which the Chicago millionaire's daughter
turns down the Grand Duke and marries an ex-
newsboy. Such spectacles, we are led to infer, are
peculiar to America alone. The implication is
that drama of this species is as definitely American
as crooked baseball and that it is unthinkable in
any other country. These other countries, pursues
the implication, are culturally above such low stuff
and are therefore represented only by drama more
or less exalted in theme and dignified in treatment.
All of which constitutes a second round of critical
buncombe. If the American drama every once in
a while gives us an exhibition that shows its author
to be, in the matter of viewpoint, taste and manners, apparently on a level with a fish merchant or
newspaper society reporter, the drama of England
and the Continent presents us with similar dishes
quite as often. For every American play that
thematically exalts impertinence and decries civil-
ity, there is an English, German or French play
that does the same thing. That these other plays
are sometimes better written should not obscure the
single point at issue, to wit, the matter of intrinsic
thematic nature. Thus, if a play like "Is Zat So?",
in which a prize-fighter and his manager invade a
home on the Avenue, conduct themselves like longshoremen and are held up as God's noblemen, is to
be accepted as typical of American drama, there is

no reason that I can see why an equally vulgar play like Zangwill's "We Moderns" should not be accepted as typical of English drama, or equally vulgar plays like Dregely's "The Well-Fitting Dress Coat," Bischitsky's "His Excellency Max," and Basset's "My Friend, the Assassin," as typical, respectively, of Hungarian, German and French.

Such generalizations are, of course, childish. There is, true enough, much thematic vulgarity in American drama, but there is also an equal share of thematic vulgarity in the drama of England and the Continent. What deceives the critics, it seems to me, is the nature of the characters through which this vulgarity is expounded. These critics assume that because the hero of a vulgar American play is, say, a shipping clerk and the hero of a vulgar European play, let us say, a painter, the latter play is therefore the less vulgar of the two. They are deluded by the labels. What the British and European criticisms of some such play as a George M. Cohan comedy are like, we know. But I should like to see the criticisms if Mr. Cohan, without changing a line of the dialogue or altering a single scene, were to print a line in the cast of characters after Kid Burns' name specifying that he was related to the Duke of Manchester or one after Hit-the-Trail Holliday's saying that he was a graduate of the University of Leipzig and an admirer of the judicial philosophy of Johann Gottlieb Heineccius.

If I seem to argue from merely so-called popular plays as opposed to drama of a higher stratum, it is because the alien critics themselves always argue from such plays. When they estimate American drama, they conveniently leave out almost all that is worthy in that drama and consider only such popular plays as will best support their contentions. The popular drama of any country is a vulgar drama because vulgarity and popularity are synonymous. But one can no more judge a nation's drama by its popular plays than one can judge a nation's literature by its best sellers. To those English critics who believe the opposite, it may be suggested—one fears somewhat ironically—that the most popular of all London plays in the last two years has been the vulgar "It Pays to Advertise" which, incidentally, was written by an American.

"THE PLAIN-SONG CUCKOO GRAY"

§ 1

There are two sides to every dramatic critic, and he is a good dramatic critic in the degree that he is able to suppress the worse side. There never lived a critic who had seen "Hedda Gabler" twenty times and who, when it was produced for the twenty-first time, would not much rather go around the corner and look at some funny new farce, but at the same time the critic has enough respect for his calling and enough consciousness of the necessity of safeguarding his reputation to lie nobly and insist that he wouldn't. There is always, too, the predilection for good-looking actresses as opposed to pie-faces; there is ever the need punditically to apologize for relatively mediocre plays that somehow irritatingly turn out to be very amusing; there is always the obligation to urge, with convincing asperity, that some one revive Euripides and Tolstoy when Euripides and Tolstoy bore the critic to death and what he actually wishes some one would revive are George Ade's "County Chairman" and the Byrne Brothers' "Eight Bells." But as a schoolmaster can't impress his pupils and hold his berth if he shows up with a whiskey breath and his shirt-tail hanging out, so the average critic must constantly make himself behave and must conduct himself as his readers expect and demand that he conduct himself. If he doesn't, one of two things will happen to him: either he will find himself out of a job or he will find himself famous, neither of which disturbing eventualities the average critic, comfortably off as he is under existing circumstances, cares to risk.

As all criticism consists in a technical mastery of the difficult art of keeping unæsthetic personal prejudices out of æsthetic appraisal, so does dramatic criticism consist very largely in whipping the more understandably peculiar of one's personal prejudices into line with the peculiarly understandable traditions of theatrical and dramatic art. That is, dramatic criticism practised by a man who has been in harness for a considerable period of time and who knows his A, B, C's—his Aristophanes, Becque and Calderon—by heart and to the point of surfeit. To such a critic, allowing, plainly enough, that he be a fellow of fundamentally sound culture, taste and discrimination, it seems that the classic drama may, after he has said his intelligent say on the subject, properly be taken for granted so far as he is concerned and be left safely in the hands of the old maids of the Drama League and the college professors who travel around the hinterland in remunerative campaigns to uplift the yokels. The critic in question does not address himself to persons unfamiliar with the classics; he assumes that his followers are thoroughly acquainted with them. He addresses himself, as Huneker used to say of himself, to a single hypothetical post-graduate reader. And he assumes that this reader needs no diagrams, charts and other such sophomore paraphernalia of instruction, but is a man on a footing with himself. A critic of any other sort is simply a sublimated reporter or a pedagogue, and should be taken out into the backyard, given a piece of chalk and set to drawing pictures of Diderot on the side of the barn.

It is at that point in his career when the cultured and experienced critic has exhausted himself on the subject of the classics that he begins to have the hardest tussle with his wayward personal fancies. He must keep up the old bluff of having the time of his life whenever some peacock of an actor produces "King Lear" or "John Gabriel Borkman" in the hope that he may be elected to the

American Institute of Arts and Letters for his great deed, when all the while his impulse, shrewdly suppressed, is to write a three thousand word essay imploring some generous manager for the love of God to put on "Krausmeyer's Alley" again or a four-thousand one about the hot show he saw last Summer at the Casino de Paris, the one with the little blonde in it. When Georg Brandes goes to the theatre in these years of his life, he invariably picks out something in which one clown belabors the posterior of a brother clown with a slat. The last theatrical exhibit that William Archer saw, before he resigned earthly criticism forever, was Florence Mills in "Dixie to Broadway." Shaw's recent dramatic amusement, he has confessed in the public prints, has been confined to Charlie Chaplin and Harold Lloyd. Jim Huneker used to sneak out of the Metropolitan in the middle of "Tannhäuser" and gallop down the block to the theatre where George Bickel was doing his fiddle-tuning act. But do the majority of critics customarily admit these things? With a few estimable and honorable exceptions, they do not. For the most part they go on with the ancient and seemly stuff. Cursing Jehovah, they pound at their typewriters on the glory of Shakespeare. Gnashing their teeth, they cover reams of white paper with the *ésprit* of Molière. Swearing to murder their wives and children that very night, they wear out dozens of pens on the nuances of Strindberg and Ibsen. And all the time their tired hearts are down the street with Joe Cook and W. C. Fields and Al Reeves, where men are men and critics may be human.

§ 2

Our humorless college professors, third-rate authors, bad actors and magazine-cover artists who are constantly howling against humor in criticism —a humor that, to them, is synonymous with flippancy—will find, if they care to take the trouble, that fine art itself is often just as flippant as the criticism which they deride. In the midst of his finest tragedy, Shakespeare is periodically as flippant as Shaw is in the midst of his finest criticism. There is more flippancy, in the meaning of the howlers, in Mozart than in all of Huneker's criticism from beginning to end. The literary, dramatic, musical and art critic of the Kutztown, Pa., *Patriot* is not one-half so flippant at his flippantest as is Brahms' bassoon, Beethoven's flute, Wagner's "Good Friday" music, Swift's "Modest Proposal" and "Argument," Goethe's "Hanswurst's Wedding," Titian's "Sacred and Profane Love," or the entire canon of Aristophanes.

61

§3

It is the practice of a certain arm of American criticism to estimate an artist not by the best piece of work he has ever done, but by the poorest. His highest level of achievement is conveniently forgotten, and emphasis allowed to rest instead upon his inferior work. This is particularly true where the artist's fine achievement bears a relatively early date mark and where his weaker efforts belong to the more immediate present. It has always seemed to me that an artist justifies himself before the world if he produces one good thing in his life, no matter how many bad things he produces either before or after it. Yet an artist is seldom criticized from this point of view in America. Let the author of "Sister Carrie" and "Jennie Gerhardt" write so much as a single negligible article for a popular magazine by way of laying in enough money for the Winter coal and a case of decent Scotch, and a score of critics will jump on his neck and announce loudly that there is nothing in the fellow, that he has been greatly overestimated, and that the embalmer is already impatiently waiting for him in the vestibule. Let the sculptor of Lincoln turn out a couple of busts of Abram S. Hewitt and Blair Thaw, and a dozen critics will let out a sardonic cackle and shout that the fellow

is a false-alarm and should be exiled to some remote plaster-of-paris *Fabrik*. Artists are not to be
criticized thus. If they were to be, the critics
would be justified in laughing themselves to death
over the later Schumann who composed "Geno-
veva," the Ibsen who wrote the epic, "Terje Vi-
gen," the poem, "Paa Vidderne," and the drama,
"De Unges Forbund," and the God who, after
creating Galileo, Michelangelo, Shakespeare and
Napoleon Bonaparte, turned out Vice-President
Dawes.

§ 4

Dramatic criticism, at least as it is practised by
such fellows as I, has a lot to answer for. (An
admission which will doubtless be endorsed with
an enthusiastic unanimity.) It is now something
more than twenty years that the school of criticism
in question has been operating in the Republic and
discharging its fusillade of sarcasm, invective,
irony and custard in general against the type of
drama that held the American stage in its grip
when the aforesaid critical cult was born and that
maintained that hold up to a half dozen or so years
ago. This was the drama of the great mentally
unwashed, the drama of cheap viewpoint, cheap
action, cheap imagination and cheap writing. Its
confectors were the Augustus Thomases, the Charles

Kleins, the George Broadhursts, the Owen Davises and the others like them, and its schoolboy philosophies, its contemptible themes and its shoddy manipulations assiduously carried on their miserable, if successful, flirtations with the American box-office and sterilized the taste of the American public. The way of this drama was an easy one, for the reviewers of the day were given to an absurd praise of it and to writing their fingers stiff over the virtues of its craftsmen. And then, presently, as I shall show in a subsequent chapter, there came upon the scene another type of reviewer. He was an impudent fellow. And his impudence was born of the fact that all he could honestly discern in its endorsers was a posse of sublime jackasses.

This impudent fellow—I use the singular, although his number was not confined to one—had, however, at the bottom of his heart a great love for drama and a great hope for the drama of America in particular, and he made it his purpose, by way of bringing about a finer order of things, to use every weapon at his command to bring the attention of the public to the scrubby spuriousness of this other drama and to ridicule it, if possible, into the garbage heap where it belonged. Day in and day out and over a period of years he urged the newer and younger men who held the dream of

a better American drama in their hearts to be
courageous enough to plow their own field, to leave
behind them the drama of heroic district attorneys,
women secretaries who turned the tables on John
D. Rockefeller, boy politicians who made the old-
time bosses eat dirt, crooks who were reformed by
sad-eyed blondes, and other such boob appetizers,
and to devote their imaginations and their energies
to drama that had something in it above the level
of the fancy of a shoe-clerk or fashionable clergy-
man. Time passed and, lo, there dawned a
change. And out of the change some excellent
things came, a measure of drama that was a credit
to the American theatre, a measure of drama that
began to draw into that theatre a more cultured
audience than it had ever known, a measure of
drama that began to be worth serious consideration
not only on this side of the Atlantic, but on the
other side as well. But with this measure of
worth-while drama there came also an even larger
measure of drama that, for all its nobler intention,
was intrinsically quite as humorously worthless as
the drama whose place it had taken.

This drama was written by young men who, dis-
missing the heroic district attorneys and super-
sapient female secretaries and uplifted yegg-men
as beneath notice, loftily set themselves to various
species of the metaphysical drama, the drama of

ideas, the drama of philosophical inquiry and the drama of subconscious monkeyshines. Manuscripts by the gross began to pour into the theatre from the Greenwich Villages of the nation. The stage began to sag under the weight of Freud and Jung. The play-typing agencies had to lay in new dictionaries and reference books. And a new set of reviewers began forthwith to cry up the glories of the new dispensation with the same ardor that the old gang had cried up the glories of the old. Yet aspiration is one thing and realization another. And the bulk of the new American plays were discovered to be at bottom no whit more reputable than the kind that the impudent reviewer had succeeded in driving to the dump. The impudent reviewer, though, true enough, his impudence had accomplished much, thus found himself in the position of a man who had thrown out the dirty water and found the tap not working while his face was still covered with lather. He had helped to rid the American theatre of its experienced professors of tawdry hokum and he had helped coincidently to bring into that theatre a lot of young men with only ambition to recommend them and utterly without the ability to do the jobs they had with an ill-founded assurance set themselves to do.

§ 5

I believe that the theatrical managers have a legitimate complaint against the manner in which the newspapers operate their play reviewing departments, and that the groans they periodically lift are not entirely without just cause. If a newspaper were to assign its art critic to review an exhibition in the Anderson Galleries one day and the $2.50 oil paintings in Gimbel's cellar the next, it would be reasonable to suppose that the editor in question was even more balmy than the average, and that the Gimbel ambassador would have the full sympathy of the public if he went down to Park Row and shot him dead on the spot. Yet we are asked to accept it as eminently proper when a newspaper does that very thing in the instance of the theatre. The newspaper hires a man as dramatic critic on the score that the aforesaid man knows reputable drama when he sees it, and likes it. Then, having hired him and instructed him to reward reputable drama with his commendation, it assigns him to review plays that, in three cases out of five, quite honestly make no more claim to being reputable drama than a Hollywood movie actor lays claim to being offspring of Saint Anthony.

That this is unfair to the managers who put on
these plays and who offer them as sound drama
no more than Gimbel offers his two dollar and a
half blobs as fine painting, should be obvious to
anyone. If a manager produces a piece of rubbish in the sole hope of making a lot of money out
of it, and frankly admits it, I hardly see the justice
in a newspaper's sending someone around to report that it is too bad he didn't produce something
by Romain Rolland instead and lose his shirt.
The usual answer to this is that the manager in
point does not admit that he is simply out to make
money, but lowers his voice in imitation of Winthrop Ames, runs his fingers through his hair like
Max Reinhardt, spits on the floor and announces
that he is hot for art now and forever. This answer is well taken, at times. But not always.
For one producer like Mr. Belasco who wishes the
newspapers to believe that even when he puts on a
"Canary Dutch" he is doing it in the name of the
good, the true and the beautiful—and who hence
fairly brings down upon himself the newspapers'
hoots—or for one like Mr. John Golden who gives
out innumerable interviews announcing himself to
be the cleanest thing the world has seen since the
invention of open-faced plumbing and hence the
saviour of a stage threatened with the filth of
Hauptmann, Rostand and Benavente, for each pro-

ducer like these you will have no difficulty in naming one who throws no bluff at all, who puts his
plays on the market exactly as some other business
man puts his gents' underdrawers, who no more
argues that those plays are anything but boob-
traps than the underdrawer impresario argues his
underdrawers are ermine opera cloaks, and who,
accordingly, deserves the same courteous treatment
that the newspapers show any other business man
and large advertiser. But do the newspapers afford this producer that treatment? They do not.
They cause his hogwash to be subjected to the same
standards that the offerings of such a producer as
Arthur Hopkins are subjected to. They cause that
hogwash to be reviewed by the same critic who,
only the day before, has announced that nothing
short of Björnsterne Björnson can keep him in his
seat after nine o'clock. They cause the poor fellow's honestly promulgated hickpricker to be
jumped on and kicked half to death by a reviewer
who has bought Theatre Guild bonds, who spends
the Summers with Pirandello and who gets a red
nose crying every time he sees a picture postcard of
Stratford-on-Avon.

There is, however, a second answer to this, to
wit, that a reviewer should be of such a catholicity
of taste that he is able to praise Porto-Riche to the
skies one night and still the next night be able to

write of Mr. Louis Kaufman Anspacher with comparative moderation and understanding. If such a reviewer exists, I have never enjoyed the honor of a peek at him. There are, true enough, men on the newspapers who valiantly try to straddle the two chairs, but they are less sound and valuable critics of drama than small-time vaudeville equilibrists. To any man of taste, intelligence and critical honor, such a straddling is objectionable, distasteful and dishonorable. There is only one way to criticize an art and that is to criticize it from the top down; to praise what is fine and damn what is bad, to proclaim merit and consign demerit to the infernal regions. This being as it is —in other words, since it is impossible for a decent critic to be at once respectful to sound drama and to commercial slops—it seems to me that, in fairness to a considerable portion of our theatrical managers, there is only one thing that the newspapers can do. That thing, that plan, I herewith offer to them gratis. Let the newspapers hire not one dramatic critic, but two: one a man of culture, experience and taste to review one kind of production; the other, an everyday bonehead with enough skill to write a readable article to review another kind. Then, let the newspapers call up the managers before the opening of their new plays and ask them which of the two reviewers they wish as-

signed to report upon the plays. The plan, I believe, would work to everyone's satisfaction. The
managers could have no complaint; readers would
know at a glance the critical viewpoint; there
would be happiness in every box. No longer
would the J. Ranken Towses of journalism be compelled to say that "The Green Hat" isn't to be
compared with "Iphigenia at Aulis"; no longer, on
the other hand, would the reviewers for the
tabloids be compelled to say that "Iphigenia at
Aulis" isn't to be compared with "The Green Hat."
We should behold the dawn of reason and of
equity, and Al Woods might at last buy himself a
new hat.

§ 6

The esteemed and valuable *Nation* lately conducted a series by American writers answering,
in the light of their personal experiences, the question: Can a literary artist function freely in the
United States? From those of the articles which
I have read, I deduce that the American writer—
Dreiser excepted—concludes that the attempt to
free his æsthetic *geist* in the Republic is about as
difficult a job as avoiding the itch in a sailors' bed-
house. It appears (*1*) that the literary artist gets
no sympathy in the United States; (*2*) that he

meets with actual opposition; (3) that the spirit of the country is against beautiful letters; (4) that the country is possessed solely by thoughts of money and has no soul; (5) that a Puritan attitude toward life makes free artistic functioning impossible; (6) that blue-nosed censorship soon disgusts the sincere and honest craftsman; and so on through 7, 8, 9, 10 and up to 495. The arguments need not be further rehearsed; they are perfectly familiar. And what is in them? After due deliberation, I believe—absolutely nothing.

For all the circumstance that now and then some lodge of smut-smellers descends upon a first-rate, or approximately first-rate, book and makes trouble for its publisher, the fact remains that there is little more moral interference with the literary artist in America than there is, or has been, in many European countries. For one reputable author who has been pounced upon by the moralists, you will find a dozen who are simply dirty boys and who deserve what they get. It is these who let out the loudest yawps on the narrowness and bigotry of the country. The first-rate author generally contents himself with a snicker and perhaps a sardonic *mot* or two, as he knows full well that it will not be long before a higher court will reverse the decision of the indignant magistrate and that, as a result of the publicity he has got,

his book, when put on sale again, will earn him
an Hispano-Suiza instead of merely a second-hand
Saxon. If there is a first-rate book by an American author that, whether at one time suppressed
or not, isn't on public sale today, I do not know
its name. The Cabells and Dreisers and Ander-
sons are each and all once again in the book-
dealers' show-windows soon after Sumner has enjoyed his fleeting hour of triumph; the Greenwich
Village geniuses with their mink heroes and rab-
bity heroines are, fortunately, not. And it is the
latter who strum ceaselessly the ukuleles of their
indignation, let loose rich abuse against the so-
called provincialism, hypocrisy and ignorance of
the country, and take the steerage for la belle
France and two-sous *Schnapps*.

There is no more opposition to the literary or
dramatic artist, and no less appreciation of his
talents, in the United States today than in any other
country. There is always a measure of such opposition; there has always been a measure of such
opposition. As a matter of fact, it is this very
opposition that has helped the cause of beautiful
letters. If the United States were a nation of one
hundred million Otto Kahns, each eager to help
art with many dollars and more speeches, I daresay
the sum of worth-while novels and plays wouldn't
be one-third what it is today. Literature and

drama are as often the product of challenge and defiance as they are of patronage and pats on the back. "Main Street" is a defiance and a challenge; "Babbitt" is another; "Arrowsmith" is another; "Jurgen" and most of Cabell are others; Dreiser is of defiance all compact; "Winesburg, Ohio," is a defiance; Eugene O'Neill is challenge and defiance from stem to stern. You will find defiance in some of the best of the early Robert Herrick and in the best work of such more worth-while of our later-day playwrights as Anderson and Stallings. Among the younger generation, defiance has produced the only literature that has been worth its bindings: such things as Dos Passos' "Three Soldiers," Smits' "Spring Flight" and Harvey Fergusson's "Capitol Hill." The finest poetry produced in America in the last twenty years is from first to last the fruit of opposition and a defiance of the popular philosophy.

All countries, as I have observed no less than 8,623 times, are in the mass much the same. The literary and dramatic artist would have just as much to grumble about in England or Germany or France as he has in the United States. Fine literature and drama, like vintage champagne, are for the few, and there are such appreciative spirits in America as there are in any European country. The truth about the matter is that the literary and dramatic artist has altogether too soft a time of it in the present-day Republic. If there is no old and established civilization to inspire him in one way, there is a young and hansdoodlish civilization to inspire him in a hundred other ways, for in the young and hansdoodlish there is ever the infinite food of mirth and irony. If now and then some T. Everett Harré gets the moral lid clapped upon him and lets out a yell that can be heard for miles around, a score of fellows superior in devious skill get away with murder. Flaubert was prosecuted in France; Goethe could not publish one of his finest pieces of writing in Germany; Swift had a hard time of it in England. In the United States of today, the only literary gentlemen who are experiencing any trouble at all are the Maxwell Bodenheims.

§ 7

When we denounce a man for mountebankery, we often overlook the fact that a touch of charlatanism is necessary to an honest, sincere and first-rate man in the Republic if he is to get his message, whatever it may be, across to the millions of boobs and blockheads who hem him in on all sides. The completely honest, sincere and first-rate man, save he practise a measure of mountebankery,

75

stands no more chance of attracting attention in the United States at the present time than a completely above-board politician or a new Haydn. A few men of his own sort will recognize him and his abilities, but the great mass of the people will remain wholly oblivious of him. To get the ears of this great mass, the first-rate man must speak to them (and conduct himself toward them) as a second-rate, third-rate or even tenth-rate man. By this hocus-pocus, due to the circumstance of like liking like, he may contrive to obtain their attention and, having obtained it, to unload gradually into their temporarily diddled heads what forthright ideas he desires to. It matters not what kind of first-rate man the first-rate man in question happens to be. He may be an artist, a writer, a musician, a critic, a financier, an editor, a business man or perhaps only a street-hawker of toy balloons, rubber tacks, smell-bombs, imitation cockroaches and busts of Theodore Roosevelt. But, whatever he is, a degree of quackery is vital to him if he would sell himself and his goods or ideas. There are men who are born frauds; there are others who have fraudulence thrust upon them. The former are not worth tobacco juice; the latter are often deserving of the highest and most intelligently critical respect.

§ 8

Millions upon millions of words have been written about "Hamlet." Critics have expressed themselves eloquently on one side of the philosophy of the drama and, when that side no longer interested anyone and didn't pay any more, with equal—or even greater—eloquence on the other. So far as I can make out, "Hamlet" is the easiest play in the world to write about, because anything you say about it seems to be true. It doesn't matter much which point of view you take; one seems to be just as sound as any other. What's more, the crazier the point of view, the surer some one will presently come forth and announce that you, and you alone, have at last hit the nail on the head.

§ 9

As a man grows older, his emotions steadily decay and, with their decay, his capacity for the fun of the world synchronously grows less and less. Ever a posturer and dissembler, he seeks solace and apology for himself in the philosophy that, as his emotions stale, his mind becomes sharper and clearer and that he thus is able to laugh sardonically at the world's show and what the world, jack-ass that it is!, believes he is missing. But there never lived a man who in his heart didn't know that the experience and wisdom of age, however blessed with the gift of ironic contemplation, were a poor substitute for certain of the emotions of which age has robbed him. Every time a philosopher over fifty buys himself a new necktie or has his shoes shined, he betrays himself for the quack he is. Wisdom, contrary to our friends, the rev. clergy, doesn't bring happiness. At most, it brings but a pseudo-happiness; it bequeathes to the mind only that happiness which it has stolen from the heart and the body; it converts actuality, with all its pungency, into mere memory and fancy, with all their impotence.

Emotions fade in the case of man just as noise fades in the case of the soldier. The thrilling racket of life's gun-fire gradually makes less and less impression upon his inured tympanum. A starlit sky, a pretty girl, a 100-pound tarpon, a Sousa march, a shooting motor-car, the enchant-ment of Southern seas, a rough-house at Dutch Sadie's, a tramp through the woods in the rain, a French farce, a set-to with the bouncer, a new checkered waistcoat, an introduction to Rabelais, a straight flush, the Place de la Concorde in the Springtime, another pretty girl, the first thousand dollars, an achievement in triumphant repartee, around in par, an initiation into the Elks—the original kick inherent in each of such transcendental emotional phenomena diminishes year by year. And with the diminution man's capacity for making an ass of himself, which is to say, man's capacity for enjoying himself, grows weaker and weaker. The moment a man becomes permanently sensible, that moment does biology snicker, quote Daudet, and buy itself a drink at his expense. The moment a man begins to say that he can now see through the emptiness of youth's pleasures, that moment is he himself most transparent.

§ 10

Among the critics of the drama in regular and active practice in the Anglo-Saxon yoshiwara to-day, it seems to me that there is one who stands out from all the others like a sprig of fresh green mint from a julep. That one is the Englishman, Walkley. Since the retirement of Shaw from the British circle some twenty-eight years ago, there has been no one to offer him serious challenge. Several vital and eloquent voices, true, have lifted themselves against the grisly routine: C. E. Montague and John Palmer among them; but the vitality and eloquence, admirable as they have been, have for one reason or another lacked staying power, and have died out, after a brief spell, from the scene. The voice of Walkley, on the other hand, has been consistently clear and resonant for something like three decades. And it has been a voice that has uniformly had in it, unless I am greatly mistaken, the most thorough theatrical and dramatic common-sense that has been heard in England or America in its time.

I do not forget Walkley's late colleague, the estimable and engaging Archer. Archer was a cultivated and experienced critic; he did some excellent and valuable pioneering; his judgments were often sound and stimulating. But as between the two men, the choice presents little difficulty. Archer's attitude toward the theatre, due to the fundamental nature and disposition of the man himself, was ever that of the professor. (What was "The Green Goddess," in sooth, but a professor cracking a class-room joke?) He approached the theatre intelligently, but his intelligence was largely set to a fixed pattern; it lacked the warmth and fluidity so necessarily a part of the biology of dramatic criticism. He looked into the theatre, in our colored friends' phrase, from the outside in—like a university don with his eye to the keyhole of a peep-show. He followed the gipsy caravan in a dress suit. He understood, and understood well, the drama, but he did not understand so well, because it was not in the soul of him to understand it, the theatre. Walkley, gifted with all the qualities that Archer had, has been gifted, to boot, with a cosmopolitanism of psyche and a metropolitanism of taste that have given him a roundness, a fulness, in the contemplation of drama and the theatre not possessed by his late lamented associate. Archer was a theory criticizing the theatre; Walkley is, in a figurative manner of speaking, a theatre criticizing a theory. His mind is a stage, brightly illuminated and suavely draped, whereon dance with sunny and lagerish smiles a hundred comedians casting hither and thither their sagacious and penetrating banderillas into the flanks of whatever species of critical bull happens to be prancing around the ring at the moment. There is ever the quality of the theatre and the feel of the theatre in Walkley's criticism, as there is and has been in the criticism of every man whose writings on the theatre have been worth any attention. In the criticism of Archer, one got this feel of the playhouse all too seldom; one got the impression, rather, of a confusion of the theatre and the library.

It isn't that Walkley does not take the theatre seriously. It is simply that, like a man with the woman he truly and deeply loves, his very seriousness makes him light-hearted, happy and gay. Beauty makes idiots sad as it makes wise men merry. Men laugh with the things and persons that are closest to their hearts. But because the rank and file of critics believe that there is something wrong with the kind of critic who, understanding thoroughly a thing that they themselves do not so thoroughly understand, takes that thing with a pleasantly careless whistle and the jaunty, sauntering swing of a cane, Walkley has often been looked on with disfavor, and favor been bestowed instead upon the kind of critic who would wear a long face at a Ladies' Day in a coon Turkish Bath. This is always the fate of a critic who knows his job so superlatively well that he can turn it inside out. The ideal critic of the multitude is not such a critic, but rather one who knows only half of his job and who conceals his lack of knowledge of the other half by taking seriously what he does not know, and writing of it even more seriously.

Walkley is not profound, in the common interpretation of the term, only in that he does not elect to be profound over matters that are intrinsically not profound. He senses the ridiculousness of sweating to build up complex theories that so little as twenty or thirty years later—thus fitful, since Aristotle lifted it out of its cradle, has the drama been—will be quite as empty and useless as an old tooth-powder can. He appreciates that the theatre and drama are as shifting as the sands of the sea and that, in that very shifting, lies the true secret of their golden, sunlit beauty. The basic laws, everyone knows; there is no need to write of them. But the by-laws change constantly; one may write of them interestingly, but, as of things that are ever in process of change, at best with an air of dubiety and evanescence, and perhaps the flicker of a snicker. "The Frogs" is a good play; "Hamlet" is a good play; "'Seven Keys to Bald-pate" is a good play. That's that. Try to fit them to the same, definite, positive, unvarying dramatic theory and go crazy in the attempt. Theories are for the class-room; drama is for the theatre. Walkley is a critic of culture, experience and sensitiveness and, being such a critic, knows just two sound standards of judgment, to wit: *1*. Whatever interests me is good; and *2*. Whatever doesn't interest me is not good. The critical technic of critics of the Archer school, on the other hand, runs thus: *1*. Whatever is good interests me; and *2*. Whatever is not good does not interest me. The subtle difference between these criteria of appraisal is the signal difference between Walkley and his contemporaries, both as critics and as men. Walkley is a personality; his contemporaries are, most of

83

them, just persons. Walkley is a positive agent; the others are positive-negative. Walkley is a cool syllogism; the others are indeterminate symposiums of prejudice, prejudgment and the dusty critical bibles of the past.

Walkley's "Dramatic Criticism," a slender little book made up of lectures delivered at the Royal Institution about twenty years ago, has more sober sense in it, to my way of thinking, than any treatise or volume on the same subject published in its time. (This statement includes Croce from stem to stern.) His various collections of dramatic criticisms, "Playhouse Impressions," "Drama and Life" and certain portions of his more recent books such as "Pastiche and Prejudice," "More Prejudice" and "Still More Prejudice" contain, also to my way of thinking, the soundest criticism of its kind that has been published in English since Shaw, though, as I have said, Montague's and Palmer's work, on a considerably smaller scale, is not to be sniffed at. The criticism of Walkley is not only shrewdly discerning and fundamentally common-sensible; it is, in addition, eminently readable and eminently charming. It also has its own share of beauty. And this beauty that it has is the genuine beauty of a tonic point of view and of a great love of life and of an easy and gracious personality, not the spurious beauty of literary pretension with which certain other critics, both in England and America, seek vaingloriously to deck out their critical nonsense. There is more good sense and more delightful reading in a casual critical essay of Walkley's than in any half dozen of the professorial flowerpots. As a critic, he is the most convincing, persuasive and attractive actor off the Anglo-Saxon stage.

He is not without his faults, of course. He has rolled a log or two in his time; he has now and again, for all his cosmopolitanism—and he is by all odds the most cosmopolitan critic in the England of his day—disclosed himself to be exceedingly insular (like most Englishmen, there is little in America that seems to him to be any good); he has been curiously anæsthetic to some of the most noteworthy advances in the art of scenic design and stage production (he has never been able to judge accurately and fully the experiments of such men as Gordon Craig, for example); he has at times permitted politeness to stand in the way of sharp and forthright execution. And, in later years, he has periodically descended to the promiscuous and very awful present-day British habit of following up an excellent critical essay with one of those mild Lamb-like papers on the lark singing outside the bedroom window in the early morn or on the toothsome pasties one can find at the Sign of the Galloping Cuckoo. Thus, in "More Prejudice," we find much first-rate critical writing interspersed with the kind of essays on blackbirds, lipsticks and letter-writing, to say nothing of a day at the Zoo, that Englishmen have been writing ever since they laid poor Elia in his final resting place these ninety-odd years ago. There is only one compensating circumstance in Walkley's case. He can make even such gimcrack subjects interesting.

A. B.—as they call him across the pond—is personally perhaps best to be described as a British James Huneker. To the late Lord Jim add a measure of British reserve, picture a mind that resembles a placid hillside stream rather than a leaping, sparkling waterfall which splashes everybody for miles around, and substitute a filet of sole Bernaise and Sauterne for a platter of sauerkraut and Pilsner—and you have Walkley. Otherwise, the two have much in common. The same multiplicity of interests, the same genial raillery, the same easy familiarity with everything from what Beethoven said to Rochlitz to what Steve Donaghue said to his barber, the same intense and warming humanness, the same broad acquaintance with everything from the best Paris restaurant wherein to get snails cooked in absinthe to the best place in Constantinople to get a shoe shine, the same winking and humorous eye, the same simplicity, the same it's-all-beautiful-but-what-the-hell's-it-all-about quality—these are Walkley's as they were Huneker's. Like the latter—God rest his companionable and deeply missed bones—Walkley is interested in everything and gives a tinker's dam for nothing. He has found that greatest of all secrets to human happiness: the philosophy of indifference. And like all indifferent men, he has a rare zest for and relish of life and the things of life. The smell of the footlights in London and the smell of the salt in Brightlingsea, the rhythm of Shakespeare and the rhythm of a pretty girl's legs, the latest star actor at the Adelphi and the newest monkey at the Zoo in Regent's Park, the Duchesse de Langeais and the impresario of tipples at the Garrick Club, Marcel Proust's *"A l'Ombre des Jeunes Filles en Fleurs"* and the shade of a Chaumontel pear tree in a quiet English orchard —fact and fancy, fancy and fact, reality and illusion, illusion and reality, these are all equally close to him—and all one. And infinitely diverting. And of utterly no importance.

Like Huneker in the matter of certain other of the arts, however tired Walkley may periodically be of the theatre and drama, he never gives the faintest sign of being tired of criticism of the

theatre and drama. He may fall asleep at a play,
but his criticism of the play will be thoroughly
wide-awake and lively. He has the gift of making
the uninteresting interesting, and—what is obviously a deal more important—of making the
worth-while and interesting doubly worth-while and
interesting. He writes with the mind of a full-
flowered man and the heart and spirit of a kid.
His method is to maintain an elaborate and amused
pretense of playing tag with a subject and having
great difficulty in catching up with it and shouting
"You're *it!*" when all the time he could do it very
simply and readily merely by reaching out his
hand. It is his favorite diversion to run after a
subject with slow-motion paces and to pass the
subject, which seems simultaneously to be moving
at top speed, before it goes half a block. He is
privy to Huneker's trick of making the reader believe at the outset that a very simple problem is an
extremely difficult one and then convincing the
reader shortly thereafter that he is a master-hand at
cracking the toughest nut. This, as in Huneker's
case, is the playboy side of the fellow. He likes
nothing so much as to tie a tin can to the tail of a
theory that his brother critics are disposed to pet
and fondle. He is, in short, like all plausible
critics, a showman. On the way into the main tent,

first and foremost there are some fetching side-shows.

If the requisites of a first-rate critic are a sound admiration for fine things, a hearty contempt for spurious things, and a rich gusto in conveying his discrimination, the one way or the other, to his readers, Walkley, Arthur Bingham, is such a one. He lacks the blacksmith directness and originality of a *Saturday Review* Shaw; he lacks the enormous cultural background of a Huneker; but one can't have everything. Shaw has left the field, and Huneker has left the earth. There remains, in control of the English-American scene, this wise and engaging, this superbly perceptive and very infinitely charming little gentleman of London.

§ 11

I am often asked why I have never written daily reviews of the theatre. The answer lies in the overwhelming amount of balderdash that is produced each season. The writer of daily reviews is compelled by the nature of his job to write extended comment on wholly worthless exhibits, and my genius is insufficient to master the technic. I can say all I have to say about such plays in one word, and no newspaper in America would print the word.

§ 12

At intervals of every few weeks, there arises
from among the people of the theatre an indignanto
of one species or another who looses the oratorios
of his wrath upon the critics of his chosen art and
proposes that they one and all be thrown without
further ado to the hyenas. During each season,
dramatic criticism and its more or less skilled professors are thumbed down no less than a hundred
different times and by umpires ranging all the way
from theatre managers and producers to actors
who appear on the program under "Townspeople"
and impresarios of trained cockatoo acts. Not
the least rococo of these various spasms was one
lately vouchsafed the readers of the daily journals
by a leading metropolitan producer who declared
that all the New York critics should immediately
be retired on pensions and that the present writer
should be made to lecture to them daily from three
to three-thirty on the fundamentals of their craft,
presumably—since the producer made no mention
otherwise—gratis. While not ungrateful for the
compliment, despite the gentleman's veiled insinua-
tion that my time and services are worth nothing,
I am yet constrained to believe that his views on
dramatic criticism as it is locally practised wear,
in part, uproarious whiskers. These views I need

90

not rehearse in detail; they have been promulgated so frequently in the past that they are long since familiar. They concern, in brief, the valuelessness of dramatic criticism as the New York newspapers exhibit it, the personal motives that often disfigure it, the damage it often works to theatrical enterprise, and so on. That there is a considerable measure of truth in the charges the producer makes, I do not presume to deny. But the mistake he makes lies in denouncing as dramatic criticism something that is actually no more dramatic criticism than the newspapers' shipping news is a novel by Joseph Conrad.

With a minimum of distinguished exception, what appears in the New York newspapers is not dramatic criticism at all, but an amalgam of hotel news, flirtations, genial backslappings, bread and butter letters and *quid pro quos* that calls itself dramatic criticism. True enough, this hotel news, these flirtations and backslappings and bread and butter letters and tits for tat are deceptively swathed in the externals of dramatic criticism, but the lingerie fools very few, and them only momentarily. To anyone who has familiarized himself with the inside workings of the *ars critica* on the home grounds, half the notices of plays and players which appear in the newspapers may be accurately foretold the day before and, in some instances,

several months before. It is relatively easy, for
example, to foretell exactly what kind of notice any
one of sixteen particular young actresses or any
one of eight or ten particular older actresses will
get. And it is equally easy to guess in advance
just how five certain playwrights will be praised
or, at worst, gracefully let down, just how the productions of two specific producers will be over-
praised, and just how the axe will be swung upon
the necks of certain unfortunate creatures, chiefly
members of the Actors' Fidelity League. As I
have said, there are exceptions which are immediately recognizable, but in general the so-called
critical reactions to local theatrical phenomena follow more or less the punch-clock I have hinted at.
If you doubt it, write me a letter denouncing me for
a doodle, for instance, the next time Miss Laurette
Taylor, Miss Winifred Lenihan, Miss Helen
Gahagan, Miss Margalo Gillmore, Miss Clare
Eames, Miss Peggy Wood, Miss Lynn Fontanne or
any one of seven other such reviewers' pets gets a
bad notice, or when Miss Margaret Anglin, Miss
Ruth Chatterton, Miss Francine Larrimore, Miss
Charlotte Walker, Madame Olga Petrova, Miss
Emma Dunn, Miss Irene Fenwick or Miss Doris
Keane gets a good one—in either case, whether they
deserve it or not. I mention trivialities, to be sure,

but straws show which way the lemonade goes. And there are many such.

Dramatic criticism, of course, is a rooster of somewhat different plumage. The producer's contention, however, that dramatic criticism which denounces an "Abie's Irish Rose" (which thereupon blissfully proceeds to run on for years) is *ipso facto* poor dramatic criticism is as jocose as the contention that because the same school of criticism praises "The Way of the World" (which promptly closes), it is therefore poor dramatic criticism. But here, of course, I get into a morass of platitude. The business of dramatic criticism has no more to do with the box-office than the business of sewer inspection has to do with art. The business of dramatic criticism is, very simply, with drama as an art and the moment it concerns itself with drama in any other way it ceases to be dramatic criticism and becomes either journalistic reporting or mere Rialto cheese-mongering. Now, it so happens that any critic on a New York newspaper who would insist upon considering drama purely as an art would promptly be booted into the street without further ceremony, and rightly. A daily newspaper is no more the place for such criticism than a monthly magazine, say, is the place for weather predictions and reports of fires. The reader of a daily newspaper is vastly less interested in the way "Aloma of the South Seas" differs from the "Heracles Mainomenos" of Euripides than in learning how closely the thunderstorm in Act II resembles a Belasco effect and how warm the cooch dance in Act I is.   To argue that, even though this be true, it should be the duty of a newspaper to inspire the reader, through its dramatic critic, to meditations more lofty is akin to arguing that it should similarly be the duty of the newspaper to uplift itself and its readers by placing its art critic in charge of its comic strips and its music critic in charge of its cabaret news.   A newspaper must have a large circulation or perish.   And consideration of drama as an art interests comparatively few persons.   Drama, to ninety-nine out of every one hundred newspaper readers, is simply a pastime, like baseball, pinochle, automobiling or making gin.   It means not potential inspiration, reflection and beauty, but merely something to go to when there is no new Charlie Chaplin or Douglas Fairbanks movie in town.   And what the newspaper reader wants is simply an intelligible and preferably humorous account of its plot, of its scenery, of its relative superiority or inferiority to various current successes, of the looks of its actresses and of the way the leading man tripped over a rug on the opening night in the middle of the scene in the villa at Lake Como and landed plumb on his calypteria. The best dramatic critic for a newspaper is thus not one who is idiotic enough to criticize drama as an art, supposing him capable of doing it, but one who, appreciating the humor of his job, writes the species of dramatic criticism that is a burlesque of dramatic criticism.

It is, of course, impossible for me to say whether the burlesque dramatic criticism which appears in certain of the local gazettes is deliberate and intentional or not, but it remains that it is excellent in that it is actually this satire on dramatic criticism. To object to this burlesque of criticism, as the producer in question and other producers have objected, is a foolish business, for were the objectors successful in getting rid of it altogether they would presently find themselves doubly embarrassed by a school of criticism that might honestly call itself dramatic criticism and that, once it got under way, would and could show them, by the very nature of it, no mercy and so would leave them with their trousers down. If our newspapers were given over to dramatic criticism in its real sense, nine-tenths of the theatres in New York would be converted into ten-cent dance-halls, garages and cinema-sinks within a year, assuming, of course, that people read and understood this real criticism, which they wouldn't. But they might in time, and therein would lie the danger to the producers. Under the present régime of criticism, on the other hand, the producers are better off than they know. If the alluded-to producer's "Dancing Mothers" suffers excessively bad notices from it, his "Quarantine" profits by excessively good ones, so it is an even break for him where under a different and sounder critical régime the two plays would get equally bad notices. As a matter of fact, the New York managers and producers are lucky. Think what would happen to their Punch and Judy shows if the six leading metropolitan newspaper dramatic critics today were Dryden, Voltaire, Zola, Brunetière, Coleridge and Shaw.

When our producers make the complaint against my colleagues of the daily press that some of them, being bondholders in the Theatre Guild's playhouse, are therefore naturally prejudiced in the Guild's favor against the aforesaid producers' interests, they say what may or may not be true. When they make the further complaint that, with two actresses in line for a certain rôle, they have to take the one with the Algonquin pull, even if she isn't as good as the other, unless they wish to lay themselves open to sour notices, they also say what may or may not be true. And when they make the still further complaint that unless they worm their

way into the personal favor of the reviewers by
hocus-pocus of one sort or another, such as seeking
advice on actors, beseeching a conference over a
play manuscript, *u.s.w.*, they will receive treatment not so kind as that vouchsafed a more proficient hocus-pocuser, they say, too, what may or
may not, for aught I know, be true. But, even so,
they bark up the wrong tree. They alone are
responsible for the present state of affairs. They
have produced the kind of plays that have given
birth to the kind of play reviewing which they howl
against. Criticism follows quality, as it leads lack
of quality. Let our producers devote themselves
to the production of sound drama and in time
respectable criticism, whether anyone reads it or
not, will inevitably and humbly follow. The producer of a "Dancing Mothers"—although I say it
who shouldn't, after the compliment he has paid me
—may have to pass out free lunches and choice
cigarros to get good notices, but the producer of
a "What Price Glory?" can always get notices ten
times better though he hand out never so much as
a three-fer and politely tell all the boys to go to
hell.

§ 13

Young men tell the truth much more than older

men. As a man grows older, he grows more and more hypocritical, and embellishes the truth with pretty and convenient knicknacks of this or that sort. He has to, if he would get on comfortably in the world, for the world has an axe out for the persistent and unashamed truth-teller and is not loath to swing it. The young man is full of impudence, courage and indifference and doesn't particularly care if the world makes him comfortable or not. But the older man thinks of his wife, his family, his neighbor, his business, his standing in the Mystic Shrine, the man who rides downtown with him in the subway every morning and his old Uncle Felix, now down with acute anterior poliomyelitis as a result of an indiscretion in "The Black Crook" days, and, so thinking, he carefully dresses up the truth in pink baby ribbons. If all the men in the United States over the age of sixty were to begin to tell the truth as Ed Howe, for example, presently tells it, granting them the ability to tell it as Ed does, the graveyards would soon be chuckablock with tombstones inscribed *b. circa 1865.*

§ 14

Criticism is the art wherewith a critic tries to guess himself into a share of an artist's fame.

§ 15

The Triumph of Criticism.—Over a period of eighty years, hundreds of critics have been laboring to improve the taste of the American people in music, literature, drama and politics. And today, as a result, Nevin, Tobani and Tosti are program favorites over Brahms, Beethoven and Bach; James Oliver Curwood is thirty thousand times more popular than James Branch Cabell; Anne Nichols is fifty thousand times more popular than Hauptmann; and Calvin Coolidge is President of the United States.

THE AMUSEMENTS OF HOMO SAPIENS

Of all living creatures, the human male mammal is the most pitiable in the matter of devising pastimes for himself. The games and diversions that man invents for the pleasure of his leisure hours are of such an unbelievable stupidity and dulness that it is impossible to imagine even the lowest of God's animals and insects indulging in relatively imbecile relaxations. Surely it would take a pretty imagination to conjure up the picture of a donkey sitting up half the night trying to find a rectangular piece of heavy coated paper with red or black spots on it to harmonize with four similar pieces, or of a bedbug going into the dining-room while a dozen other bedbugs in the parlor think up the name of Gutzon Borglum and then returning to the parlor and trying to guess it.

The diversions which man relies upon for the gratification of his spirit are, in point of fact, infinitely more fatuous than those upon which the lower animals rely. When a dog, for example, wishes to disport himself and forget his cares, what does he do? Does he sit in a stuffy room with a number of other dogs and strain his eyes laying out little tiles with Chinese figures on them, the meantime carrying on a conversation about the relative merits of Beluga and Astrakhan caviar and the superiority of Eddie Davis' jazz band to Emil Coleman's, or does he very intelligently curl up in a corner, take a squint at the human idiots, grunt and go into a good, comfortable snooze? Or take a guinea-pig. When a guinea-pig claps his eyes on a lady of his set who moves him strangely, does he put on a boiled shirt and a butterfly tie, sit around with her for six hours in a French restaurant owned by an Italian and run by a Greek, periodically get up and, with her, bump his anatomy against a hundred other anatomies to the tune of a wind instrument with a derby hat hung on the end of it, and subsequently ride around the Park with her in a taxicab without any springs, or—I ask you, gentlemen,—does he not?

A horse, in his moments of play, runs around a beautiful green field, eats a bit of delicious, cool, green grass and lies down under the spreading shade of a tree and lets his imagination dwell upon a score of presumably lovely fancies. A man chases a small round hunk of gutta-percha for three miles through a series of mudholes, patches of poison ivy and cow-streams and then, after engaging in some dubious mathematical calculations, guzzles half a pint of henna'd wood alcohol. And so it is with the other merriments of animal and man. When a goat wants diversion, he eats a *New Republic*, plays with some tin cans, and whinnies. When a man wants diversion, he reads a *New Republic*, listens to a jazz performer play on the same tin cans, and sings "Dixie."

Consider, for example, the manner in which the average human being mellows his psyche in the theatre. What is the nature of the stimuli that he finds to his taste? First, there is the Chinese play. This consists of an old Sardou manuscript with Scarpia dressed up as a Chinaman and with the scene laid in a Shanghai bordello that resembles nothing so much as an all-star revival of "Florodora." For about five minutes before the curtain goes up, one hears the gifted MM. Feinbaum, Schultz and Riesenberger, of New York Local 61 of the Musicians' Union, making what is supposed to be Chinese music. An inside curtain embroidered with dragons and something that looks like herring salad is then allowed to beguile the audience's eye for another five minutes, during which time various colored lights are thrown upon it by way, presumably, of manufacturing the true Shanghai atmosphere. When this second curtain is eventually pulled up, a cloud of corner drugstore incense is blown out at the customers, setting up a wealth of Occidental bronchial disturbances. Then slowly the lights go up and, after about fifteen minutes of unintelligible pidgin English on the part of several girls in silk pajamas, the star actor enters in a green kimono and smoking a long pipe, gives forth a few ominous grunts, and the great art work is on. We now duly behold the fair Tse-Tse with the strain of Caucasian blood, the loveliest hussy in all the Orient. We behold the sinister Chang-Lo who comports himself with the grim imperturbability of a deaf embalmer, who covets the fair Tse-Tse's marble body and who vows that death will be the portion of any white dog who thinks to take her from him. And we behold our old camarado, Cavendish, the Englishman whose girl back home has done him dirt, who has come to the Orient to forget, who strains the fair Tse-Tse to his bosom and who awakens in her the tremors of a soulful love.

Then there are the other sex barouches in which country girls are led astray by the squire's dissolute nephew; in which Henri Pathétique, the venerable sausage manufacturer, discovers that his wife has betrayed him with Raoul Capricieux, the young painter; in which the maid is seduced by the son of the household; in which the betrayed peasant girl learns that her beau is a cad at heart and declines in an impassioned speech to accept his proposal of marriage; in which the stenographer tearfully confesses to Courtney Van Rensselaer Gooseberg that she cannot become his wife because in the long ago she surrendered her chastity to a Yale sophomore; in which clergymen succumb to the lure of ex-ballet dancers and opera singers; in which the big scene consists either in a ringing defense of sex or a ringing denunciation of it; in which the young man on trial for stealing the ruby suspender buckle turns out to be the illegitimate son of the prosecuting lawyer and in which, a moment later, the old scrubwoman of the Criminal Court building turns out to be the culprit's mother; and in which amorous ancients lock the door and demand that their fair supper companions step up and deliver.

Not forgetting the plays in which two-hundred pound quondam actresses sneak away from their stodgy husbands for one last wild fling at Budapest night life and subsequently picture their moral dissolution by drinking half a glass of champagne and singing the chorus of a French song; in which a sex-starved young woman has an affair with a handsome Austrian lieutenant and thereafter goes around looking as if both her parents and all her brothers and sisters had been killed in a railroad accident; in which Equity actors in white grease paint prove the corrupting languor of the tropics by carrying on with Equity actresses in brown grease paint; in which young Jewish boys sentimentally give up $75,000 a year jobs in order to work for nothing in their deceased fathers' old pants shops on the East Side; in which the juveniles imagine that they resemble the Prince of Wales on the score that they have blond hair, own a double-breasted gray suit and fasten their collars with a gold pin; in which young actresses, in turn, imagine that they can pass for Duses by brushing their hair straight back from their foreheads, smearing their faces with white chalk and going in for a wealth of monkey-business with their hands, also smeared with white chalk; in which a cheap interior, a few calico wrappers and a rented piano pass for a profound study of suburban life; in which the actors drink a magic bolus, tell the truth for an hour and a half and then, the effects of the occult *Schnapps* wearing off, revert again to normal; in which aged criminals break into houses on Christmas Eve and discover that the houses are none other than those of their long-lost daughters and that the child-actors jumping around the Christmas tree are their own grandchildren; in which character actors, following the theatrical conception of all Germans over the age of fifty, shake their heads up and down after every sentence; in which other actors in white wigs who limp about the stage, periodically take off their spectacles and wipe them on their sleeves and who are able to speak three words in any foreign language are hailed as great artists in character delineation; in which a Scotch Cinderella with ankles like Benedictine bottles winds up in fine feather at the Laird's ball; and in which the innocent mother, driven from the house in Grosvenor Square years ago by a husband who accused her of infidelity, fights against the latter for her son's love and in which the kindly, grayhaired old family confidant seeks with mellow worldly wisdom to bring pity and understanding into the cruel husband's heart—not forgetting these, we must list also the creams which are made to pass for historical drama by stationing an old Negro butler at the upper entrance and causing him periodically in a loud voice to announce the entrance of various notables of the period such as Martin Van Buren, John Quincy Adams, Henry Clay and Daniel Webster, whereupon enter in turn as many supers made up to look like William McKinley, Senator Borah, Theodore Dreiser and Dudley Field Malone who bow profoundly and take up their starchy positions at stage right and left; in which actors' idea of characterizing

Frenchmen is to throw two-fingered kisses into the air every other minute by way of expressing ecstatic admiration and actresses' idea of depicting French-women is to spend several thousands of dollars on Paris gowns, put them on and then spend the evening pacing rapidly back and forth and up and down the stage as if the play were designed pri-marily as a means to relieve cramps in their legs; and in which an iron-willed and obdurate ancient is gradually reduced to humility by the object of his wrath, usually a young girl, and in which there are offered, *seriatim*, the vociferous 'stigmatiza-tion of the heroine with a word that is not cus-tomarily employed in polite society, the scene in which a lascivious fellow demands the heroine's body as the price of his services in her behalf, the child who clings lovingly to the heroine's skirts when the latter is sorely beset by the other members of the family, the old sailor who periodically stops stock still, sniffs the air and mutters symbolically about an approaching storm, the patient, plodding wife who stoically suffers her husband's brutal turpitude with a brave, sad smile, and the hard old farmer to whom crops are everything and to be set above his womenfolk's happiness.

Further, we engage the plays with the proletarian hero who fears not heaven, hell or king and with the aristocratic heroine, blonde as a wedding-cake

107

and regal as a burlesque queen, whose resistance
slowly melts in his strong embrace; the plays in
which the balcony spotlight, as big as the head-
light on a Baltimore and Ohio locomotive, illu-
minates the spectacle of a swordsman in a lace
shirt putting to rout single-handed a hundred
dollar-a-night supers and sending them bumping
pell-mell down the stairs like so many Saratoga
trunks; and the mush-mills in which all the men
in the cast, save two, appear with their bodies
painted a rich russet and clad only in short
B.V.D.'s—the exceptions appearing in white linen
suits and pith helmets, in which the leading woman
is made up to look like Little Egypt, and in which a
supper-club steel guitar quartet periodically inter-
rupts the proceedings with some wail *Musik*. These
are what are known as South Sea Island plays.
The hero is a young Caucasian, outfitted by Aber-
crombie and Fitch, who has fled to these parts to
escape the haunting memory of a false sweet one
and who is in the first stages of delirium tremens
when the curtain goes up. The heroine is the
usual ingénue in the string of beads and with a
large bandanna wrapped around her Back Bay
whose physical comportment suggests that she has
swallowed a trapeze, who talks like a Choctaw
Peg o' My Heart and whose naïve innocence and
sweetness of soul gradually reclaim the hero from

moral dissolution. Then, too, there are the sinister native who would safeguard the little heroine, Balona, from the predatory white man; the girl from back home in the white dress and with the white parasol who shows up just as the hero has declared his intention of making the native maiden his lawful, wedded wife; the drunken, amorous, good-for-nothing husband of the girl from home who is duly killed off in time to clear the way for a happy ending; and a number of supers stripped to the buff who are given such names as Luana, Moana, Unola, Nahoma and Boano and who mosey in and out of the action muttering "Wahee." There are also the inevitable steamer *Venturia* with its passengers from San Francisco, including the girl beloved of the hero before he went to the dogs; the battery of off-stage electric fans that whips up the window curtains at the end of the second act by way of presaging the terrible tin-sheet pounding into which the villain is due presently to go out and lose his life; the scene in which the little native maiden speculates cutely on the morals of the white man, with the hero gathering her hungrily into his arms at the conclusion of the monologue, whispering hoarsely, "Let them say what they will, the hypocrites; you are in my blood, my veins; you drive me mad; I love you!"; the fight in which the hero saves the little Balona from the advances of a drunken sailor, knocking the latter over the head with a papier-maché bottle seized from a convenient table; and the scene in which the little native maiden, with many a cunning *moué* and arch titter—"me too like white lady, see!"—tries on the habiliments of civilization.

Continuing the catalogue that entertains the image of God and that brings ecstasy to his soul, we discover the play in which an actor in a gray wig and with a crick in his back bargains with the devil for the soul of a young man, drinks a potion, sits for a tense moment in the crimson glare of the fireplace, and presently gets up feeling like Jackie Coogan. After two hours spent in learning that youth, after all, is youth and age is age, the actor sips a second seidel, sits for a tense moment in a stream of green moonlight, and totters to his feet feeling again like Chauncey Depew. Also the play in which an actor in an Inverness coat and with talcum powder all over his face, and who speaks like Israel Zangwill, is supposed to represent Jesus Christ; the melon in which an aged artist achieves happiness by sitting in his darkened studio and conjuring up the vision of some one whom he has loved in the dear, bygone days, the vision being embodied for theatrical purposes by a small-salaried actress in a blonde wig embellished with a rose, who from time to time

110

somewhat noisily crawls out of the fireplace, takes her stand back of an elaborately carved chair and is illuminated by a baby spotlight; the straight mystery play which the author has been unable to sell and which in despair he thereupon calls a burlesque of mystery plays and with a great show of sophistication then presents to the public; the locally manufactured Irish play with its Owen Davis plot retailed by characters arbitrarily named Padna, Eileen, Sheila and Corny and with its Connecticut happenings shifted to a locâle designated in the program, if nowhere else, as a seacoast village in the County Clare; the jewel in which a woman opens a door leading into a room where a man and a girl are, falls back with an exclamation of horror and an expression indicative of the beholding of an act of adultery and subsequently reveals that all she saw was a hug; the exhibit in which the leading man, in the rôle of a novelist immersed in a book that must be finished without delay, comes out of his workroom every fifteen minutes with a doggy new suit on; and the play in which the irate father starts out to bribe and unmask the girl his son is engaged to and learns that she is really a very decent sort—to say nothing of the Methuselah in which the leading characters are flabbergasted to find that they are occupying neighboring private supper-rooms in the same restaurant; in which the son, the worse for liquor, coming upon his father in the company of an obvious woman, tempestuously accuses his father of doing the very thing of which the latter has accused him; in which the second act curtain falls upon the ejaculation, "Well, I'll be damned!"; in which comedy is extracted from a scene in a café between an old beau and a flashy chorus girl; and in which the daughter, called to accounts by her parents, retorts that she didn't ask to be born. Nor must we overlook the *comédie larmoyante* in which the dead baby's little worsted shoes bring the husband lugubriously to forgive his erring wife; the nonesuch in which the flapper fails to recognize her own mother in the bachelor Lothario's chambers because the mother's back is turned; the proud confection in which it is proved that if a very young girl marries an old man she will soon or late feel stirring within her certain suppressed impulses; the one in which the heroine conveys to the hero that she is with child by looking steadily at her shoes; and the epic in which a forty-eight year old Broadway star, in the rôle of Aurélie de Belleville of the Comédie Française, is revealed in the prologue in a Little Eva makeup, coyly plays peek-a-boo behind the chairs, impetuously shakes her false blonde curls and otherwise leads old Papa Duval relevantly to observe that she will some day grow up to be a great actress with all Paris at her feet and who is duly disclosed in the last scene—Papa Duval's prognostication having been already fulfilled—in Shakesperian costume and a white wig tottering off-stage to claim the thunderous plaudits of an imaginary audience in the wings. This last play may further be identified as the one in which the star actress goes through the usual rigmarole with her various lovers, two or three dozen of whom volunteer to go to the ends of the earth if she will but deign to permit them to so much as presume to kiss her hand; negotiates the divers elaborate shenanigans supposed to be symptoms of artistic temperament; bears a boy child that is impersonated, first, by a child actress who resembles Baby Peggy, then in later years by a youth who resembles Siegfried Sassoon, and finally in his mature years by a member of the Actors' Equity Association who resembles Henry Seidel Canby; boxes various presumptuous persons' ears and the next moment rushes up to them and contritely embraces them; has so large a retinue of servants that the manager of the show nightly comes near dying of heart failure thinking of the expense; and casually refers to kings, queens, dukes, duchesses, earls and marquises as her intimate friends, with now and then a sharp dig at one or another of them by way of showing how simple of heart and democratic she really is.

In the way of military exhibits, we observe that the subject of our discussion has found enchantment in plums like "The Heart of Maryland," the theme of which deals with the saving of the Confederacy by a trapeze act; like "The Conquerors," the idea of which consists in the hypothesis that a lady who has fainted does not know, after recovering consciousness, whether she has been raped or not; like "The Girl I Left Behind Me," in which the white actors, besieged in a stockade by Indians and doomed to be scalped and quartered within the next two minutes, while away the time by writing letters of farewell to their dear ones (said letters presumably to be mailed by the obliging Indians after the slaughter); and like "The Flag Lieutenant," obviously produced only because some London matinée idol fancied the way he looked in a naval uniform and because some unimaginative playwright thought it would be a fine idea to have a brass band play the national anthem off-stage as the final curtain fell. Then, too, there have been the palpitations in which Sepoy villains are struck down by cobras just as they are about to knife British majors; in which English heroines dive off paste-board men-o'-war in order to get dispatches to Downing street in time to baffle malevolent and vaguely identified forces; in which fifteen supers in uniform circle around a backdrop painted to resemble Trafalgar Square thirty or forty times by way of convincing the yokels that they have paid in their money to see a "mastodonic production"; and in which an Irish-American sailor of the United States battleship *San Jacinto* pulls the whiskers of the visiting British admiral and airily recalls to him certain *contretemps* of 1775 and 1812, with the parting shot, expressed both verbally and with chewing tobacco, that what we done once we can do again. In another direction, there is the idyl in which the elegant Armand Valry lures the beauteous and flighty heroine Mozella to his rich bachelor boudoir, there to visit his wicked will upon her, and in which his trustworthy man-servant Yamamoto always exercises the usual precaution of leaving the front door open when his master is engaged in esoteric amours, that the fair Mozella's husband may come upon the lovers in the nick of time; the one in which members of the Actors' Union run around the stage half naked and smeared with butternut oil shouting something that sounds like "Ohio Weehawken Oolong" in the fond belief that they are being regarded by the audience as natives of Tahiti, and the one in which Robert B. Mantell in Santa Claus getup with a gilt curtain-pole in his hand endeavors to persuade the same audience that he is Lear, king of Britain; the one in which the heroine's guardian tells her, in a voice so tearful that even the press-agent breaks down nightly and cries like a child who has been kicked in the stomach, that he loves her as he does because he once loved her dead mother who, alas, rejected his suit in favor of another, the latter turning out to be none other than the knave who has stolen the young woman's inherited share of the silver mine; the one in which the wild bird found imprisoned in a cage is symbolically released by the hero; the one in which the leading rôle, regarded as a profound character study, consists simply of an old Smithfield in a gray wig who negotiates such stencils as fits of irascibility lapsing abruptly into warm-heartedness, slow and laborious getting into and out of arm-chairs, flinty sternness alternating suddenly, as if by rote, with gentle kindness, the gradual coming on of paralysis, accompanied by the customary bull-like actor breathing, and the final repertoire of physical quiverings—all duly accompanied by such familiar lines, speeches and bits of business as the recollection of happy, bygone days—"there were actors in those days; we haven't any actors any more!", the admonition to the young folk to avail themselves of the pleasures of life while there is yet time, the smacking of the lips over good port wine, the sigh for the love that was lost, and the eventual brave exit without regret or qualm; the polite drawing-room comedy in which the front door-bell is heard to ring like a fire alarm every time a visitor calls; and the boon in which an octogenarian composer finds the inspiration for his greatest symphony in his landlady's flapper foster daughter.

But is the spirit of *Homo sapiens* satisfied by these alone? It is not. Adding to the gratification of his nocturnal marrow is the trump in which a revolver shot is followed by the hero's cool wrapping up of his hand, and, upon the heroine's agonized solicitude, by his nonchalant remark, "It's only a scratch"; the one in which the hero magnanimously sends the misled youth out to his ranch in Montana—"It'll make a man of you, my boy"—and the youth's impulsive grasping of the hero's hand with "You're dead square, Mr. Gundersdorf, that's what you are, dead square! I'm ashamed of myself, ashamed of what I've done. I promise you you won't regret this; you won't be disappointed in me"; the melodrama in which Captain Greville Sartoris, with the connivance of Madame Petoski, the Russian adventuress, tries to prevent Bluebell from winning the Derby; the circumbendibus in which a young husband separated

from his wife through a misunderstanding calls
on her on her birthday and, telling her that his
rich uncle Herman from Peru is about to arrive
for a short visit, beseeches her to act during that
time as if nothing had happened between them,
that the rich uncle may thus be kept in ignorance
of their estrangement—the wife agreeing and the
subsequent pretense of the young couple leading
to their eventual happy reunion; and the play in
which Horace Terhune anticipates fame through
the production of his opera, in which Horace's
sweetheart, Gervaise de la Tour, a famous prima
donna who is due to sing the leading rôle in an
opera by Horace's rival, Edward Dubois, is coveted
by the latter, and in which it is eventually discovered that the rascally Dubois has stolen Horace's
manuscript and palmed it off as his own. Also,
there is the morsel in which the convicted hero is
saved from the electric chair at the last moment
through the discovery that the dead man was not
murdered at all, but died from the blow suffered
when, upon learning that Desmond Rosenblatt was
still alive and in New York at the moment, he
fainted in his library and hit the back of his head
on the brass railing around the fire-place; the so-
called polite comedy which relates the marital
vicissitudes of a couple of smartly dressed actors
—one of them, of necessity, a popular star—and

the manner in which the husband and wife, separated for the second act, are duly brought together again in the third; the sweet in which a young girl of transcendent innocence comes by a baby without knowing how or why; the play in which the heroine shrinks in horror from the kiss of the Italian count whom her family insist she marry, takes the hand of the clean, manly young American and tells him that, when he returns from the oil fields a year hence, she will be waiting for him; the imported balderdash put over on the intelligentsia as an expressionistic-impressionistic melomonodrame by the great Firmin Katzenjammer; the mystery play in which the supposed murderous ghost turns out to be an un-insulated electric wire that the villain has placed under the banister of the stairs leading to the spot where the treasure is secreted; the one in which the demise of the unscrupulous capitalist is revealed to have been accomplished by a small automatic revolver concealed in the fountain pen with which he made out the receipt for the Swiss Hand Laundry bill; the one in which doors in darkened rooms mysteriously open without any human aid whatsoever save a visible black string pulled by a stagehand whose shadow is clearly discernible against the wall just outside; the one in which the bumpkin who has apparently been frightened half to death throughout the evening and who has indicated that fright by an elaborate chattering of teeth and quaking of knees turns out in the end to be none other than Inspector General O'Halloran, the great Scotland Yard detective, to the surprise and huge amazement of everybody in the theatre but the audience; the one in which the book-case is seen slowly to move, the while the arm of the knavish Emil St. Cyr, thickly smeared with whitewash to make it look spooky, steals forth from behind it either to remove the pistol from the escritoire or to lift the necklace from the throat of the heroine sleeping upon the chaise-longue; and the one in which the romantic crook who steals the priceless Rembrandt does so not for the value of the painting but for the intense æsthetic gratification he derives from works of art.

Not less pleasurable than any of these, we may believe, is the play in which the portrait of the late and sinister Maurice Watz occultly falls to the floor with a crash when his name is mentioned; the Oriental drama which consists of several hoochie-coochie dances periodically interrupted by invocations of Allah and by processions of actors, camels and goats dressed up like so many "Follies" girls; the melodrama in which a horse race, locomotive or fire engine is dragged into the action when the plot gives out; the one-act play which the

author spreads over three hours by getting the maid
to answer the door-bell and serve tea in terms of a
slow-motion movie; the elixir in which the actors
come close to the footlights and excitedly describe
a horse race presumably going on in the back aisle
of the theatre; the play professing to tell the story
of Judith and Holofernes which is merely a chroni-
cle of the Adventures of Phallus in Wonderland;
the play whose prologue discloses a Falstaffian old
gentleman with gout and glucosuria from too great
indulgence in rich foods and vintage wines and
which then switches back twenty-five years in Act I
and asks its audience to get excited because he is
apparently about to die of starvation and thirst in
the desert; the play in which the detective cleverly
gets the suspected crooks' finger-prints by upsetting
the inkstand as if by accident and in which the
dégagé crooks, when alone on the stage, descend
to the hully-gee form of speech; the one in which
a buxom *tuberculeuse* breathing out her last upon
a bed of death suggests fibroid phthisis infinitely
less than indigestion from a dozen or so filets
mignons and apple strudels; the one in which a
character designated in the program as "an eminent
neurologist" dictates to his secretary his latest and
most profound contribution to the world of patho-
logical thought, which contribution makes even the
osteopaths out front laugh; the one in which some

Greenwich Village genius dramatizes the Strindberg philosophy of hate-in-love by making the husband periodically clench his fists and stride abruptly toward the window for a relieving breath of air and by making the wife periodically clench her teeth and stride snappishly out of the room with her tummy thrust forward at an impertinent bulge; the play in which the heroine apologizes for her misstep in terms of her restrained and starved youth, numerous moist allusions to the need of poetry in a woman's life and references to the Italian hills in the April sunlight; the one in which the leading man believes that modish nonchalance may be indicated by never standing up straight and by rolling back the coat lapels to display a fancy waistcoat; the play about Rome in its glory, with all the Romans looking like General von Hindenburg in a nightshirt and with a tin soup-can on his head and the yelling in which is so loud that for blocks around the neighbors conclude that the theatre has gone broke and that an Eighth Avenue dentist has taken over the building and moved in; the play in which the leading woman, determined to be a stickler in the matter of clear diction, enunciates all words ending in *s* like so many sister Susies sewing socks for soldiers; the epigrammatic comedy with gems like "A good woman is merely one who hasn't had any temptations"; the screwdriver in which, at the beginning of the first act, the hero narrowly scrutinizes the suspicious-looking butler and observes in an ominous whisper, "Hm! I seem to have seen that fellow somewhere before"; the balsam whose author believes that the surest way to make the audience feel sentimental is to make the dramatic characters feel twice as sentimental as the audience; the risqué play containing the high-minded and moral actress who recites the lines allotted to her as if they were so many distasteful lozenges; the Broadway opus close to the heart of star actresses which gives them a chance to recite bits of Shakespeare, that they may prove to their audiences how excellent they would be in the classics if a cruel fate didn't condemn them to the sort of things they are currently appearing in; the otherwise dull milch-cow into which the producer tries to inject a little life by sprinkling the text with local allusions and names, much as Lew Dockstader used to bolster up his monologue in the hinterland towns by sticking into it a reference to the mayor and the name of the biggest local saloon; and the emprise in which a gentle con man takes the burden of his illegitimate daughter's guilt—she has shot the man who tried to seduce her—upon his own shoulders and without revealing his identity to her permits the gendarmes to lead him *dolentemente* from the scene. Nor must one overlook the one

containing the line, "There is no creature more
foul than he who steals a child's faith"; the one in
which a rain-storm or disabled automobile forces
the hero and heroine to spend the night in a deserted farmhouse, to the subsequent scandalizing
of the heroine's puritanical fiancé and maiden
aunt; the one in which an unmarried couple find
to their dismay that the innkeeper has only one
bedroom left; the play in which a humdrum married man longs again for adventure and freedom,
leaves his wife and child for Bushwah, Nassawara
Province, Central Africa, there comes to realize
that he is not as romantic and youthful as he had
thought, and returns again to his home in Saginaw,
Michigan; the one in which an artistic producer
seeks to achieve realism by causing a group of
supers at stage right to chatter *sotto voce* about
Dodge automobiles, the latest quotations on genuine
Scotch, Count Salm and other such relevant topics
while the leading characters at stage left are con-
ducting the author's dialogue about the coal strike
in Lancashire; the one with some such title as
"Daddy Dumplins" which contains a scene in which
a beatific fat man crawls around the floor with
three child-actors astride his back; the patriotic
French war play which looks upon war much in the
light of a panorama of Barbara Frietchies, Florence Nightingales, Sousa marches, bronze statues

and then to deliver themselves of such observations as "If all this happened on the stage, no one would believe it"; the one in which a rich young man falls in love with a poor working girl, plans to make her his mistress, but, upon learning that she is a good girl, begs her forgiveness and asks her to be his wife; the one in which a married woman, in order to cure her husband of the lulu of whom he is enamoured, throws the couple constantly into each other's company and thus causes the husband to tire of the hussy and return to her a better and wiser man; the one in which a young woman, in order to beat the terms of a will, marries a supposedly aged man on the point of dying and in which the latter not only does not die but removes his white wig and throws away his crutches and reveals himself to be a very handsome young dog; the one in which a New York luxury-loving young married woman tries to play with fire without getting burned, comes near singeing herself, is repentant and plans with her husband to leave the city, live in the country and mend her ways; the one in which a scarlet woman comes face to face in later years with the man whom she loved in the days of her sweet and innocent girlhood and struggles to keep the secret of her past from him; the one in which two young lovers whose families are bitter rivals in business profess to

love the mates whom their respective families have
picked out for them and eventually flabbergast
their families with the news that they have been
married for a year and have a bouncing baby boy,
the latter being the means of bringing about a
reconciliation and forgiveness; the one in which
a girl is betrayed by a married man and in which
her father, learning of it, is mad as hell; the one
in which a husband who is a stern moralist seeks
to prevent a young man from marrying a woman
with a blot upon her name, learns presently that
his own wife suffers a similar blot, and thus has his
eyes charitably opened; the one in which a
sagacious butler smooths out a family's difficulties;
the one in which a poor old mother whose son has
made a lot of money is installed in an elegant
house but is unhappy there and longs to return
to her small tenement room; the one in which a
divorcée falls in love with a married man but
realizes that if they go away together it will mean
great unhappiness for the man's wife and therefore gives him up; the smutty farce in which
seventy-eight *double ententes,* one hundred and
thirty left-handed dodges, one hundred and eighty-
three circumlocutions and an equal number of
synonyms are laboriously employed to evade the
direct use of the word fornication; the one in which
the rôles of kings, crown princes, royal chancel-

130

lors and dukes are played by members of the Lambs' Club; the one in which the boy and girl brought up on a deserted island learn the secrets of sex from the birds, the bees and the flowers; the one in which a popular male star of 1870 plays the rôle of a passionate young Spaniard; the adaptation in which a French chorus girl lives platonically with the man she loves; the one in which Marie-Claire feels in her heart the call of her beloved Montmartre; the one about the noble and upright young governor and the political plotters laid in a room in the State capitol with the usual oil painting of Cyril Maude above the fireplace; and the other adaptation from the French in which a bachelor finds a pretty girl in his bed and therefore tiptoes quietly out of the room and goes to sleep in the arm-chair.

GENIUSES

The discovery of new great geniuses goes steadily on. Not a month passes that one or more such *Wunderkinder* are not dredged up from this or that corner of the world and presented with a staggering tooting of trumpets and rattle of drums to the hitherto dumb-bell Corinthians. Every other ship leaving Havre and Cherbourg has on board a cargo of critical articles from the Café du Dome telling of new and amazing performers in the arts, said articles invariably accompanied by photographs of semi-bald little gentlemen with rather soiled goatees. Every other ship from Bremen or Hamburg brings with it at least a gross of critical essays heralding the discovery of astounding talents, said essays duly accompanied by photographs of young men with brushy pompadours and with expressions on their countenances presumably suggestive of the grief of a stricken nation. And every other ship from Southampton and Liverpool has on it a trunkful of critical papers proclaiming divers fellows gifted with the divine fire, said papers accompanied by photographs of either tousled-haired, horse-faced gentlemen of middle years in mussy soft collars or sleek younger men with movie-actor moustaches and figged out in latest modes in wing collars and bat-wing ties. All these articles, essays and papers, with the photographs in question, appear shortly after their arrival in the *Dial, Vanity Fair* or the *Theatre Arts Monthly,* and a month or so later, in but slightly altered form, in the literary and dramatic pages of the Sunday newspapers.

Genius, No. 4,629, one of the latest to arouse the local æsthetic tongs to flights of ecstasy, is the Frenchman, Charles Vildrac, author of the three plays, "Le Paquebot Ténacité," "Le Pèlerin," and "Michel Auclair." The M. Vildrac was discovered by the local branch of the International Great Genius Discovery Association, Inc., a few years ago, coincident with the branch's first visit to the Latin Quarter of Paris and with its first taste of *ecrevisse* and Byrrh. The initial reports of his overpowering *geist* came, if I mistake not, from the M. Waldo Frank, to whom every Frenchman who has read "Rahab" is reciprocally a dazzling virtuoso. And no sooner had the foxy M. Frank planted his banner on the beach and claimed Vildrac in the name of God and Greenwich Village than a dozen or more young associates tumbled promptly out of the Algonquin and the Mad Hatter and lifted up their voices to heaven in acquiescence. At the beginning, the apostles were content to acclaim their new saint simply on the score of his extraordinary performances in the arts, the said extraordinary performances then consisting chiefly of one play, "Le Paquebot Ténacité," and a small book of war poems, "Chants du Désespéré." But gradually the saint took on other and even greater (and perhaps more significant) virtues; and thus presently we find the M. Frank saying of him that "there is no better guide than he to the profound restaurants of the *Halles*." Indeed, the M. Frank may be said to give himself away rather affably when he observes of Vildrac that "when you see him . . . you think of lovely tables and of wine . . ." (One is glad to learn that Charles himself is unquestionably privy to the humors of such occasions, for Frank alludes, albeit in apparently perfect innocence, to "the twinkle in his eye so serenely bright.") As the months have chased one another, however, Vildrac's disciples have thrown all reserve to the winds and have come out flat-footed in declaring that not only are his dinners excellent, but that he himself—I quote the M. Sidney Howard—is "the most arresting writer for the theatre of France of today, and probably the most important Continental dramatist now living. It must indeed be a rare genius which

. . . can create so definite and exalted an impression!" and that—to quote still another enthusiast—"his 'Le Paquebot Ténacité' is the outstanding play of the contemporary French theatre."

Recovering somewhat from these bomb-shells, which blow up completely the rank pretensions of such Continental dramatists as Hauptmann and of such contemporary French plays as "La Dernière Nuit de Don Juan," let us consider briefly what manner of dramatic genius this latest find of the local art neckers is. Of "Le Paquebot Ténacité" I have spoken in the past. It is a smoothly written and very leisurely ironic comedy with an obvious theme containing an adroitly handled scene of seduction and some character drawing of an obvious though periodically amusing sort. It is not quite a so-called full-length play, theatrically speaking; it has moments of drama and of grace, and moments wherein dulness is the wages of an insufficiently fertile dramatic imagination; it is, from any level of authentic criticism, at the very best a third-rate achievement. "Michel Auclair" is similarly not a full-length play, again speaking in terms of the contemporary theatre; it is even more leisurely than "Le Paquebot Ténacité"; it is a reading play rather than an acting play; it is, so to speak, undramatized. And it is, as a play if perhaps not as a literary manuscript, excessively flat. It is a short story set upon the stage, little more. "Le Pèlerin," a one-act play, fails to stir up even Vildrac's loudest bally-hooers; it may be dismissed. What we thus find, in sum, is an agreeable but very mild theatrical talent whose intent is the achievement of drama through a simple perception of life simply trans-lated to a theatre stage but whose actual achieve-ment remains the simple perception of life in-effectively filtered through the sieve of drama. In "Michel Auclair," for example, Vildrac's real-istic simplicity is theatrical and dramatic zero. His characters, figuratively speaking, sit around and complacently devote themselves to talking about the play he should have written. The theme of "Auclair" and that of "Ténacité" are at bot-tom one and the same: the victory of the physical over the sentimental in love, and the inevitable beauty that may lie in the sometimes cruel and ugly heart of the former. But Vildrac remains an incomplete dramatist. He states his theme clearly; his characters go through the paces of relating the theme; but the air is ever sultry with the technic of the story writer rather than the story teller. His characters move, but in their movement they do not carry drama with them. He sets himself forth as a realist of simplicity; what he actually presents himself to us as is a pleasant and sometimes charming minor talent that has strayed from between book covers and lost itself in the hard and dynamic glare of the footlights.

Genius No. 4,630 is, by name, Mr. Michael Arlen. The colossal admiration of the two great English-speaking nations of the earth for the literary genius of this Mr. Arlen, while immensely gratifying as an indication of improved taste over the erstwhile ichthyophagy of Nat Gould and the Rev. Thomas Dixon, would yet seem to indicate that the Anglo-American æsthetician has still some distance to go before he will be able duly to appreciate and prostrate himself before the even more remarkable literary genius of such fellows as Edward William Poel and Mr. Rupert Hughes. But the future is in the future's hands, and the present is Mr. Arlen's. One hears his eminence shouted from the housetops and the roofs of jazz palaces; one sees his volumes on the tables of ladies and ladies' maids; one reads of fêtes in the great man's honor at all the movie studios, supper clubs and breakfast flapjack houses. The splendor of the gentleman's waistcoats, the morsel of repartee with which he floored Mr. Adolph Zukor, the unbelievable amount of mazuma he gets for writing so much as one choice paragraph, the Cloisonné monograms on his lingerie, the Chinese jade pant-button presented to him by the Marchioness X. as compensation for the one lost in the Daimler on the way home from the Metropole "Follies"—with such news are the literary prints aburst. It was only the unfortunate accident of the M. Anatole France's death, indeed, that compelled Mr. Smyth, of the *International Book Review,* to kill one of Mr. Arlen's photographs at the last moment and thus bring out his intelligencer with but eleven likenesses of the great man instead of an in itself all too measly dozen.

The artistic success of Mr. Arlen is thus hardly open to question. Wherever one finds persons open-mouthed before the Second Hungarian Rhapsody, the "William Tell" Overture and the performances of Ukulele Ike, or eating boiled birdshot at two dollars and a half a portion under the impression that it is Russian caviar, or thrilling to the masterful prose of Gertrude Atherton, or drinking California Sauterne with a Seidlitz powder in it in the belief that it is vintage champagne, or complaining that *Young's Magazine* isn't what it used to be—wherever one finds such persons one finds coincidently impassioned devotees of the Arlen art. Seldom, indeed, in the history of more recent æsthetic phenomena has a writer been so widely acclaimed by the jazz babies and coon shouters of literary criticism. And what, one asks, is the reason, the *risposta*, the *éclair-cissement*, in a word, the *verdammte Ursache?* Let me at this juncture introduce the amazing, aye, uncanny haruspice and seer, the M. G. J. Nathan.

The high favor in which Mr. Arlen is held by the Anglo-Saxon connoisseur is the high favor that is ever the reward of the purveyor of what, for want of a politer phrase, may be termed rented dress-suit literature. In other words, the species of literary composition that smacks internally of having been born on the backstairs but that has been cunningly disguised in evening clothes, given the title of Duke, instructed to allude periodically, with something of a bored drawl, to Lake Como, the bad manners of Mayfair and the passably fair quality of the host's Emparador sherry, and brought into the drawing-room. In the last forty years there is no record of the commercial failure of beautiful letters of this school. Where literature to the manor born may find a limited audience because of a wider audience's discomfiture in its strange and to a degree alien and unintelligible presence, literature that apes literature to the manor born, that wears its lapel bloom and spats with a certain readily penetrable embarrassment and that betrays its unfamiliarity with the charming absurdity of hig-leef to the extent of taking it seriously, generally finds a brother Elk

139

in the reading public. For that public, numbering into the hundreds of thousands, is itself like that literature. When a John Galsworthy speaks to it—or even an Edith Wharton—it believes only the half of what is told it; but when a Robert W. Chambers or an Arlen speaks to it, it recognizes in the butler an old boyhood friend and grasps his hand warmly and inquires, albeit mannerfully under its breath, about the home folks. The world of Arlen's prose is the fashionable world of Mr. Cecil De Mille. And like the latter great artist he profits by its immediate recognizability on the part of the million elegantos in mufti who sit in the pits of the Kingdom and of the Republic.

It was once remarked and it has since become a platitude that the average hero of the late Richard Harding Davis was the office boy's idea of a gentleman. The average heroine of Mr. Arlen is an headwaiter's idea of a romantic lady. But though Mr. Arlen, like Davis, never fails to wear a top hat to market, he lacks Davis' very real skill as a writer. His talent lies rather in the Chambers direction. Like Chambers, he knows how to tell a story; like Chambers, he is privy to the trick of taking an ordinary sex story and making it seem romantically important to the modish yokels by laying it in tony surroundings, giving the characters such names as Major General Sir Maurice

Harpenden, Bart., and causing them to use a species of language that is a cross between the poetry of Cale Young Rice and the dinner-table conversation of an over-educated Negro; and, unlike Chambers, he has a measure of superficial humor. And so it is that he goes down the reading and theatrical public's gullet like Epsom salts. To those in that public who have less taste and relish for romantic physics of this sort, Arlen's art is perhaps more readily appreciated for what it is: a simultaneous *reductio ad absurdum* of the manner of Arthur Wing Pinero and sublimation *ad absurdum* of that of the earlier Robert Hichens. It takes cleverness of a sort to achieve such a technic, and to that extent is this Mr. Michael Arlen a clever man.

Genius No. 4,631, in turn, is, by name, Mr. Noël Coward. Since this Mr. Coward appears presently to be the figure occupying most greatly the combined attention of .English and American Solons of the drama, the phenomenon may perhaps with a mild profit be made the subject of inquiry. In London, Mr. Coward has stirred up more profound critical excitement than even the latest American Charleston hoofer at the Piccadilly cabaret. His plays have been praised in a few quarters in terms that the English critics customarily reserve for books of children's verses

by contributors to *Punch* and denounced in many
more in terms that the same gentlemen customarily
reserve for the better American novels.   He has
been dubbed, on the one hand, the most talented
writer of comedy that England has known since
the already forgotten genius who was last year
dubbed the most talented writer of comedy that
England has known, and, on the other, he has
been stigmatized, because of his themes, as the
greatest smear on the fair name of the London
stage since a translation of Wedekind was last
shown on a Sunday up an alley.   In America, Mr.
Coward has for the most part fared better.   Here,
the critical gentry has seized him to its bosom with
all the passion hitherto husbanded for Mr. Martin Flavin and the Four Marx Brothers.   Indeed,
not since Duse, pitiably ill from a hemorrhage,
gave what she confessed was the worst performance of her whole career in Gallarati-Scotti's "Cosi
Sia" at the Century Theatre, has anyone been the
recipient of such sweeping and abundant acclaim.

One of the things that seems especially to impress the commentators about Mr. Coward is his
age.   Is it not remarkable, they say, that this
young man of twenty-five or so should already
actually have written and had produced four plays
and a dozen music hall numbers?   When one politely, if somewhat timidly, hazards the rejoinder

that, for that matter, Mr. Coward's fellow English playwright, Mr. William Shakespeare, similarly had written certain of his little things in his twenties and that Mr. Coward's fellow composer, Mr. Wolfgang A. Mozart, had published six sonatas at the age of nine, one is dismissed as a fellow of deplorable wise-cracking proclivities. For we live in a critical age when a performance in the arts is rated according to its impresario's years, when the death of a second-rate poet at twenty-six is the occasion for more tears than the death of a first-rate poet at sixty, when the Nathalia Cranes steal the first pages of the literary reviews from the Robert Frosts and Carl Sandburgs, when the Phillip Barrys are eulogized in proportion as the Pirandellos are gracefully let down, and when the *Bookman,* the *Dial* and the *International Book Review* lead off with Stephen Vincent Benét and Johnny Weaver and bury Cabell and Dreiser somewhere in the back among the advertisements of unexpurgated editions of "The Adventures of the Marquis de Faublas."

Another thing that deeply moves the critics about Mr. Coward is what is described as his "keen dramatic sense and remarkable gift for theatrical effect." Analyzing this, in the light of his recently disclosed plays, what do we find? We find, first, that this keen dramatic sense of his consists

for the major part in the old trick of reducing
dialogue to monosyllables and that, secondly, this
remarkable gift for theatrical effect consists for
the same part in pumping up the aforesaid mono-
syllabic dialogue in a violent staccato to a bursting
point and then bringing it up with a sudden jerk
by causing one of the speakers either (*a*) to grab
a piece of bric-à-brac, hurl it to the floor and smash
it to bits, or (*b*) to turn on the other speaker, the
immediate subject of a crescendo denunciation in-
volving every epithet known to longshoreman and
fishwife, and with lightning-like abruptness to
make a fervent protestation of undying love.   The
dialogue that Mr. Coward writes is nervous and
terse, but its nervous terseness is less suggestive
of that of life and actuality than of the nervous
terseness of moving picture sub-titles.   One de-
tects, in one's mind's eye, the arbitrary and wholesale use of supposedly breath-taking dashes and
exclamation points.   One feels that the characters
are speaking the language of human beings not
so much as the language of a playwright grimly
determined to make a record in the way of verbal
economy.   This sort of theatrical dodge is all very
well in the kind of plays in which detectives snoop
around in haunted houses with pocket flashlights
looking for the spitzbub' who has been passing
himself off as the ghost of the murdered banker,

but it becomes travesty when an attempt is made
to employ it in high comedy. This, surely, should
be known to Mr. Coward by this time despite his
youth, for the device has served as the basis of
many a burlesque both in his own England and
our America.

Mr. Coward's act climaxes, already alluded to,
are quite as arbitrary in their ready-made effec-
tiveness as his dialogue. Nor can one find in
them much inventiveness or originality. Surely
such a device as the smashing of a piece of pot-
tery, which brings down the curtain on the second
act of his "Easy Virtue," is quite as rococo as
the theme of the play itself, both the theme and
the act climax in point having been employed
literally in the remote yesterday of the theatre by
Pinero. The dramatic climax to the second act of
another of Mr. Coward's plays, "The Vortex," and
largely responsible for the theatrical success of
that play, to wit, a crescendo musical accom-
paniment to a scene of mounting dialogue, has
similarly taken its place in the catalogue of stage
tricks since Henry Irving and the day of "Water-
loo." Passing from these phases of Mr. Coward's dramatic craftsmanship, we come to the matter of his atmosphere, as the word goes. While
never for a moment suggesting the jewelry-
salesman manner of his contemporary, Arlen, in

his effort to inject "tone" into his plays, while, to
the contrary, contriving his airs with entire ease,
acquaintance and conviction, Mr. Coward never-
theless periodically gives one the impression of
straining himself to overawe his more susceptible
auditors with divers schnitzels of the *beau monde*.
A slightly too nonchalant allusion to Marcel
Proust, a condescending voucher for the Ritz, a
titbit about this or that recherché interior dec-
orator, a reference to jade bathtubs, such morsels
as "she's giving a dreadful reception at her dreadful house for some dreadful Ambassador," with
the rejoinder, "How dreadful!", casually inserted
mentions of Debussy, Ravel, Gabriel Faure and
Reynaldo Hahn, much to-do about "Cachet Faivre"
and such like, references to fashionable Paris
couturiéres and to Caron's "Narcisse Noir" and
other currently smart smells, elaborate intimacy
with various Continental salons and watering-
places, passing mention of tennis, cricket, bridge,
mah jong, bezique, Russian music, Claridge's, the
Embassy Club and Monte Carlo, numerous calls
on our old French friend, *chic,* information as to
the vogue in Paris parlor games—these he rolls
on his tongue with something of Arlen's relish.
. . . We come, finally, to the meat of the Coward
opera. Save in the case of "Fallen Angels," which
has not yet been shown in America and which

146

contains a fresh and amusing theme, Coward seems to go regularly to the attic for the ideas of his plays. Thus, we find "The Vortex" to be little more than a paraphrase of Maugham's "Our Betters," "Hay Fever" to be an echo of St. John Ervine's "Mary, Mary, Quite Contrary," and "Easy Virtue" to be a readily recognizable grandchild of "The Second Mrs. Tanqueray" and the dozens of plays of similar theme that followed in its wake.

But if all this is true of the young man's plays, how are we to account for the attention that he has attracted on both sides of the Atlantic? Unless I am in error, this attention has been due to his stratagem of making old stuff seem lively and up-to-the-minute by the George M. Cohan dramaturgic and theatrical device of writing and playing it as if it were a cross between a special delivery letter and a hurry call for the police. One need only glance at the printed texts of his plays to catch the secret. Where the playwright of yesterday went at a Coward theme as if he didn't expect his audience to arrive at the theatre until the beginning of the second act, Coward rips off his shirt and begins pulling corks at once. He doesn't bother with preliminaries; he gets promptly to business. This, of course, is a procedure that generally brings the less meditative critic to believe that a playwright, however empty, has so much of im-

portance to say that he can hardly wait to say it
and that he feels he must begin to say it at once
if he is to crowd all his vast fund of ideas into
the meagre two hours at his disposal. I do not
insinuate that Coward himself has any such foolish idea in his head when he writes his plays, for
he gives no sign of posturing or pretense. What
I say is that Coward's critics, hornswoggled by his
cunning and practical knowledge of theatrical
guile, are brought very tidily to the view of Coward
that Coward wishes them to have. Yet Coward,
though I may seem to have indicated otherwise,
is by no means to be confused with such currently
prosperous dramatic charlatans as Arlen. Below
his obvious parlor magic, his box-office bait and his
mummer card-sharping there is discernible a talent of some mild quality. Now and then he shows
a gift for quick character analysis—there are two
instances in "Easy Virtue"; now and then he fashions a brief scene instinct with life and reality;
now and then he discloses an eye that for a moment
or two has clearly and honestly appraised human
beings in their birthday clothes. More, he is without sentimentality, and there is courage of a sort
in his make-up. If thus far he has written utterly
nothing of importance, there are yet in his utterly
unimportant plays indications that one of these
days he may justify at least a small measure of

the commendation that has already been bestowed upon him by critics who have mistaken his merely effective theatre for sound drama.

Genius No. 4,632, the next on the list, is, by name, the M. Firmin Gémier. The M. Firmin Gémier, of the Théâtre National de L'Odéon of France, invited to display the splendors of his art to the Americano by the United States government! The event held an incredible promise. A proclamation of welcome was issued and signed by such rabid apostles of æsthetics as John Aspegren, James M. Beck, Paul D. Cravath, James K. Hackett, David Belasco, John W. Davis, Victor J. Dowling and George W. Wickersham. Following the proclamation, a banquet was spread by Otto Kahn at which the guest of honor, seated between the dramatic critics for *Women's Wear* and the *Hardware Dealers' Digest*, was greeted with a dozen affectionate and eulogistic speeches, including eleven long ones by Mr. Kahn himself. There was a visit to Washington during which the French artist shook hands four times with President Coolidge, was kissed on both cheeks by the Secretary of the Navy, was given an autographed photograph by Louis Brandeis, laid a wreath on the grave of the Unknown Soldier, and was taken to the top of the Washington Monument and allowed to drop an apple over the edge to see how long it would take it to fall to the ground. Returning them to New York, the M. Gémier laid wreaths on Grant's tomb, on General Sherman's statue at the entrance to Central Park, on the statue of William Cullen Bryant in Bryant Park, on the statue of Admiral Farragut in Madison Square, and on Saks and Company's new store in Fifth Avenue. Luncheons, teas, receptions and dinners were tendered in the official visitor's honor by the president of the Board of Aldermen and by Lee Shubert, Jackie Coogan, Larry Fay of the El Fey Club, the National Institute of Arts and Letters, Morris Gest, the Columbia University football team, Jesse Lasky, Samuel Shipman, the Fairbanks Twins, Samuel Rothapfel, Texas Guinan, the Rev. Dr. Percy Stickney Grant and Ted Lewis' Jazz Band. The M. Gémier was, further, given a key to the city, a season pass to Minskys' Winter Garden, a trip around the city in the police boat, a front table in the Lido-Venice restaurant, free sittings at White's, Campbell's, Muray's and other photographic studios, six cases of Silver King mineral water, a view of Brooklyn from the Woolworth tower, a trip to the synthetic champagne factories over on Staten Island, and was taken to the Saturday services in St. Bartholomew's Church. The town buzzed with the glories of the eminent French artist for two excited weeks, and then the curtain went up at the Jolson Theatre. The play that Firmin Gémier, chief exponent of modern French theatrical and dramatic culture, revealed to his admirers was "L'Homme Qui Assassina," a melodramatic potboiler by the potboiling Pierre Frondaie out of a potboiler novel by Claude Farrère. And the play that Firmin Gémier, chief exponent of modern French theatrical and dramatic culture, next revealed was "Le Procureur Hallers," an even more melodramatic potboiler by the potboiling MM. de Gorsse and Forest out of a doohinky by Max Lindau.

But, after all, Shakespeare and Molière were announced to come later, so the M. Gémier's admirers might, they meditated, preserve their enthusiasm by giving over their attention from the plays themselves to the M. Gémier's acting in the plays and his staging and direction of them. Yet the M. Gémier's acting, they found, showed the effects of too many banquets and Otto Kahn speeches. Or something. For the performances that the distinguished visitor gave in these two plays —and, to the astonishment of all the admirers, in the Lenormand play that succeeded them, as well —were seen to be no better than the average performances that one encounters in the average Broadway production. But still, thought the admirers, there was hope. For Gémier is considered

151

to be the greatest of modern French producers. And in his productions of the plays, whatever the plays themselves and the acting might be, one would detect his true genius. Yet something appeared to be wrong in this department, too. The décor, the costumes, the direction of the stage were, the admirers reluctantly had to confess to themselves, not nearly so good as the better-grade Cleveland or Rochester stock company's. Borders of foliage that screened off the top of the proscenium as in the 1890's, houses painted on the backdrop with cut-out windows wherein cerise lights glowed, tapestries painted on the interiors and with no regard for the panel lines, polo players dressed like moving picture directors, military and naval attachés who wore what were presumably full dress uniforms not only at evening affairs but in the morning to boot, a single pair of red curtains that economically represented varied scenes in the Alps, in Paris, in Algeria and elsewhere, a single pair of brown curtains ditto, a small table lamp that cast a light as of Luna Park at the height of the season——it was rather difficult, the admirers found, to reconcile such things with the foremost producer in present-day France.

The days passed. And presently came the productions of "The Merchant of Venice," "The Taming of the Shrew" and "Le Bourgeois Gentil-

homme," each duly prefaced by the M. Gémier's
further laying of wreaths on the statue of Chester
A. Arthur in Madison Square, on the bust of Cer-
vantes in Central Park, on the statue of Garibaldi
in Washington Square, on the Obelisk in the Park,
on the Straus Memorial at Broadway and 106th
Street, on the statue of S. S. Cox in Astor Place,
on the New York and Long Branch Railroad station at the foot of Desbrosses Street, on the Y. M.
C. A. building in West Fifty-seventh Street, on the
Heinrich Heine fountain at Mott Avenue and 161st
Street, on the Sloan Maternity Hospital, on the
Colored Working Girls' Home in West 131st
Street, on the St. Joseph's Institute for Improved
Instruction of Deaf Mutes, on the Gansevoort market, and on Lüchow's restaurant. There were
also more luncheons, teas, receptions and dinners
at which the guest was welcomed anew and proclaimed the greatest theatrical genius of France
by Ed Wynn, Peggy Hopkins Joyce, Augustus
Thomas, Vincent Lopez, Montrose J. Moses, S.
Stanwood Menken, Elizabeth Marbury, Bernarr
Macfadden and twenty or thirty other international
art fanatics. And there were also, as a fitting
climax, a few additional two or three hour speeches
by Mr. Kahn. And then again the curtain went
up. The admirers, having put on fresh boiled
shirts, sat on the edges of their seats ready to

discharge their bravos. The air was pregnant with a thousand anticipations. But once more something seemed to go wrong. While slightly, very slightly, better than his antecedent exhibits, the Shakespearian plays appeared to be, at best, *tours de force* in eccentricity, stunts rather than well-composed dramatic productions, beanfeasts of vainglorious producing idiosyncrasies rather than coldly reasoned out and warmly projected dramatic works. And the Molière play showed little more to inspire the intelligently critical among the guest's hosts.

What, then, seems to be the truth about Firmin Gémier? The truth, distilled from a contemplation of his labors both here and abroad, seems to be that he is exactly what he is commonly regarded to be: the best producing director of the present-day French theatre. But in that truth lies a second truth and this second truth is that the present-day French theatre is a distinctly third-rate theatre, not to be compared, even remotely, with the German theatre, or the Austrian theatre, or our own American theatre. Gémier is, therefore, merely a big frog in a little puddle. In that little puddle his producing talents take on a bulk that in any of the other theatres I have named would not be even faintly discernible. But in his puddle, a puddle wherein the only other native

producer with even half-way modern ideas is
Jacques Copeau—Pitoëff being a Russian—he
seems comparatively something of a genius. To
say that Gémier is the foremost of modern French
actors, however, as he has been locally press-
agented, is to make a whopping detour from the
fact. He is, to put it bluntly, nothing of the kind
and, what is more, no judicious Frenchman regards him as anything of the kind. He is a fairly
talented actor, and one with a certain amount of
imagination and a pleasing presence, but he is far,
very far, from the first, or even the second, level.

Genius No. 4,633, to come finally, with a meet
flourish of trumpets, to a product of the Republic,
is Mr. John Howard Lawson. This Mr. Lawson
is in many respects a typical specimen of the little
theatre young American playwright, and so may
profitably be placed under the microscope for
dramatico-eugenesic purposes. In him, we find at
once the relative virtues, in so far as they exist,
and the faults of the considerable bevy of young
men whose dramatic impulses have been allowed
to function since, several years ago, half the
smaller garages, undertaking parlors and delicatessen stores of the Republic put in a hundred or
so chairs apiece, installed boxes with slits in them
at the front doors and announced that they were
henceforth temples of the Muse. Among the

talents produced by these *Spielschulen* were two or three of importance—the name of O'Neill stands out like a visiting star in a hinterland stock company—but for the most part what was brought forth and what still remains to decorate the scene was and is mere aspiration with a cock-eye. Such aspiration with such a cock-eye is Mr. Lawson. In him we discover the ambition of a Hamilcar and the equipment of a Salvation Army captain.

Mr. Lawson has written three plays: "Roger Bloomer," "Processional" and, most recently, "Nirvana." The first was an attempt to see New York through the eyes of a Georg Kaiser or Walter Hasenklever; the second was an attempt to translate the spirit and essence of America into jazz rhythm. Both were attempts, and stopped there. In the former instance, the eyes of Kaiser and Hasenklever were to a degree present, but absent completely was what happens to be back of Kaiser's and Hasenklever's eyes. What we got, accordingly, was Expressionism that had nothing to express. In the latter instance, a provocative and interesting idea went to pieces on the rocks of amateurishness and indexterity. The will was there, but the skill was lacking. What was called for was some such faint measure of competence as was shown by Giacosa in his indifferent miniature, "Les Ficelles," which shows us human beings dancing inevitably to the jazz strings in the hand of an invisible puppet-master, or by Birinski in his "Narrentanz," which gives us the jazz dance of European politics. That skill, Lawson was without and, as if duly appreciating the deficiency, he resorted to the not uncommon subterfuge of concealing the fact in, and distracting attention from it by, a set of exercises in freakishness. In this, he is not unlike many of his colleagues in the little theatre pidgin-dramaturgy. The latter persuade themselves to believe that novelty of theme is only to be expounded in a novel dramaturgic manner, the word *novel* being invariably regarded as synonymous with freakish. In isolated cases, it is true that a novel theme demands a novel manner of telling, but in the customary run of things dramatic one pretty generally finds that the best and most convincing way to retail a novel theme is through the more or less standardized dramaturgic method. If, for example, a playwright set out to show us that it is Satan who rules over Heaven and God who rules over Hell, his best method for doing the job would in all probability be to follow the dramatic technic of, say, Hauptmann in "The Sunken Bell," since a wild fantastic idea by no means inevitably calls upon a wildly fantastic dramatic form for its most effective exposition. Yet give one of the little

157

theatre playwrights some such idea and the first
thing he will do will be to devise a dramaturgic
structure that will play the first act, laid in Heaven,
in the balcony, and the second, laid in Hell, downstairs in the men's washroom. This is the prin-
ciple that Lawson adopts. His "Nirvana" is one
of the best examples I have seen of the lengths to
which the little theatre dramaturgic nonsense has
gone. For his basic theme, he has taken old
Pontius' query, "What is truth?" Having asked
himself that question, he should next have inquired
of himself, "What is drama?" But that is a
question such young men as he seldom ask of
themselves. Drama, to them, is anything that is
absolutely unlike what is played on the stages of
the professional theatres. Everything south of
Fourteenth Street is drama; everything north of
Fourteenth Street is not. In the instance in point,
drama, according to Lawson, is a "Notes and
Queries" department spoken aloud by actors.

A glance at Lawson's published preface to his
play reveals clearly what is wrong with him.
" 'Nirvana,' " he says, "is a comedy of the uncertainties and aspirations of the thinking man as
he confronts the enlarging universe." This so-
called thinking man is the chief protagonist of his
dramatic exhibit. What do we find him to be
like and what, consequently, do we find Lawson's

conception of the modern thinking man to be like?
We scrutinize the character's cerebral functionings
—the character may doubtless be accepted as re-
flecting Lawson's philosophical doctrines—and
find a mind which, by the Binet-Simon test, is all
of fifteen years old. It is this mind that the
playwright seriously means us to accept as one
gifted with mature, if tempest-tossed, thought; it
is this species of eristic mind that he postures
against his dramatic circumstances. Among the
things that this mind, or dramatic protagonist,
"thinks" are, quoting literally, the following: (*1*)
that a pure love and a pure faith may cure a girl
who has broken her spine; (*2*) that a woman cannot tell exactly who the father of her child is; (*3*)
that if Christian Scientists had complete confi-
dence in themselves they might accomplish what
medical science has failed to accomplish; (*4*) that
half the young women of New York are constantly
undergoing operations for abortion; (*5*) that if
the present age of machinery does not soon devise a new religion it will collapse; (*6*) that a
woman's discontent with life is invariably due to
sexual causes; (*7*) that Mars may be reached by
an aerial torpedo; (*8*) that scientists are in the
habit of surrounding themselves with perverts and
degenerates; (*9*) that a detective can mingle un-
invited and unobserved by the host or guests at

a party for sixteen people; (*10*) that it is danger-
ous for a famous and reputable physician to go
to a scene of murder unless he takes the precaution
to bring his nurse along as a witness; and (*11*)
that the work of such men as Robert Koch is utterly valueless. Of such stuff, to be liberal in the
matter, are the "uncertainties" of Mr. Lawson's
modern thinking man. It is this mind which, in
his foreword, Mr. Lawson "has desired to probe
and consider."

To continue. "What has religion to do with
this?", asks the author, and then answers, "Even
across strictly scientific thought there comes the
shadow of a new mysticism. Freud has dragged
strange monsters from the bottomless sea of the
unconscious. Einstein has deposed the straight
line." What, one may be pardoned for asking,
is precisely the shadow of the new mysticism that
has crossed strictly scientific thought? One fears
that Mr. Lawson is a student of such profound
scientific documents as Sir Arthur Conan Doyle's
"The Coming of the Fairies," to say nothing of the
works of Margery, Mary Baker Eddy and Camille
Flammarion. What is the relationship between
mysticism and our old friend Sigmund? What
spooks have been tickling Einstein's ear? "View-
ing the mental uncertainties of today," proceeds
our young philosopher, "I am convinced that there

is a religious need not satisfied by any of the current forms of worship." In other words, what is needed to resolve scientific uncertainties into certainties is a new theology. I content myself with a polite silence.

One thing, however, *is* certain, and that is that the little theatres cannot hope to develop a respectable American drama out of such monkey-shines as these. These theatres are trying to develop not dramatists so much as sociologists and philosophers, and all that they are actually developing is a troupe of absurd sophomores who are running around making faces at Pinero, Havelock Ellis, Abraham Erlanger and God and who are being patted on the back by the *Dial* and the *New Republic*. What most of the little theatres need is (*1*) an intelligent play-reader, and (*2*) a good-sized waste-basket.

THE PRINCE'S TAILOR

To demand that a critic should on all occasions go to the play without prejudice is to demand that the critic, as a sensitive human being, should not feel itchy at eight-thirty of any specific evening after twenty or thirty years of uninterrupted residence in a mosquito swamp. To ask a critic to approach a dramatic exhibit with a mind purged of all prejudice is to indicate a man upon whom culture, training, perception and experience have made and left not the slightest impression, in short, a man who takes with him to the theatre a mind as open, and as empty, as a Boston art gallery. The critic who approaches the theatre or anything else with a mind completely free from prejudice, granting that such a critic exists, is simply a blockhead and so equipped perfectly only for the criticizing of political speeches, moving pictures, radio programs and Charleston contests. Prejudice is as natural to the cultivated mind as garters are to socks. There are, to be sure, certain excellent adult gentlemen who maintain that they approach a work of art utterly without preconceived opinions, but there are also certain otherwise excellent adult gentlemen who boast that Dr. Pearl in his "Biology of Population Growth" has unbelievably under-estimated their virtuosity as *beaux sabreurs*. Prejudice is the salt of the intellect. The intelligent man is, out of the very necessity of his intelligence, a bundle of presumptions and predilections, many of them trustworthy and eminently valid. His mind, of course, is open to new ideas, new philosophies and new convictions, but they must first pass through the breastworks of the sum of his antecedent learning, reflection and deduction. The surface of his mind is open and receptive, but the under-layers are more or less tough with the lessons of knowledge and experience and with the carefully built up tissues of taste.

Thus, to expect a critic to approach an exhibition of "Hamlet" in modern clothes with his mind not pretty well made up in advance that the presentation will be ridiculous is like expecting a man to approach a circus with his mind not pretty well made up in advance that the tent will hardly smell like a bed of roses. The critic may, with a certain amount of reason, be expected to know that it will be as absurd to picture a figure out of Danish saga in the manner and dress of contemporary civilization as it would be to costume

"Is Zat So?" in the manner of the early Vikings.
To take a character out of the legend and history
of centuries long gone and to present him, and the
persons around him, as modern characters is, in
the critic's prejudice, quite as apt as the imagination that would picture Saxo-Grammaticus as the
editor of the *American Magazine* or Belleforest
as the leader of a jazz band. But it will be said
to the critic that it is less the figure out of legend
and history than the figure Shakespeare created
whom he is asked to regard as a modern figure,
and that, further, since the play of Shakespeare is
universal in its implications, there is full justice
in ridding it of the garments of a specific period
and in vesting it with those of any period, including that of today. To which the critic will quite
properly answer: *compote de pommes*. For the
critic will say that, if this kind of argument is
worth anything, he can see no reason why, if it be
pushed to its logical conclusion, it wouldn't also
be an excellent idea to dress up Shakespeare's
Richard III in khaki and a Sam Browne belt and
shift the scene from Bosworth Field to Belleau
Wood. And if the critic's retort fails to have
the necessary effect, he may take another hitch
at his trousers and inquire further wherein precisely lies the universal applicability of a play in
which a young man goes crazy because his father

has been murdered, because his mother then marries his uncle, because his best girl also goes
crazy, because graveyards are full of low comedians and because everyone poisons or stabs everyone else within a radius of fifty miles; and
wherein, in addition, lies the modernity of a play
in which intelligent people actually see ghosts and
carry on long conversations with them and in which
the same persons invite sixteen-year-old girls to
parties at which the entertainment consists chiefly
of descriptions of what goes on in lovers' beds and
of wise-cracks about incest and adultery?

Surely, the critic must be antecedently as opposed to such tomfoolery as he would be to a
production of "Ben Hur" in which Rolls-Royces
were substituted for the chariots and in which the
Saviour was made up to look like the Rt. Rev.
Dr. Manning. That "Hamlet" was presented in
Shakespeare's time in the habiliments of the Elizabethan day doesn't persuade him any more than
that men used to play women's parts in the day
of the Greeks. That Garrick played Macbeth made
up like a Knight of Pythias doesn't persuade him
of anything more than that Garrick was by way
of being something of a jackass. And that "Hamlet" is timeless doesn't persuade him that this is
any more sound reason for arbitrarily making it
timely by dressing it in modern clothes and with

such modern appurtenances as the telephone, Smith and Wesson revolvers and whiskeys and soda than there would be for making such an equally timeless play as "The First Year" more universal by taking out the telephone and the Grand Rapids furniture and dressing it after the period and manner of Louis XIV. To attempt to emphasize the universality and timelessness of a great work by ridding it of its traditional rigging and palliament, repeats the critic, is as idiotic a procedure as would be an attempt to underscore the universality and timelessness of the "Eroica" by taking out the violins, 'cellos and clarinets, putting a saxophone, a cowbell and half a dozen kettledrums in their places, and so making it intelligible to modern musical morons.

Any such dodge as the converting of "Hamlet" into a Saville Row exhibition by way of making it more intelligible must seem to the critic a brazen concession to a mob of ignoble numskulls who are incapable of appreciating anything unless it be reduced to terms of A, B, C, and who, accordingly, are worth no more consideration than so many dead fish. Surely, the person who is not sufficiently educated to understand "Hamlet" or any play like it save it be translated for him in terms of Piccadilly and Broadway and amplified with a magic-lantern slide lecture is hardly the person that the self-respecting critic addresses himself to. It is all very well for a theatrical producer to address himself to such a person, for unless the producer gets that person into his theatre he will lose money and in due time have to close up shop, but that is another matter. The critic doesn't care whether the producer loses his money or not. And it is thus that the critic, delivering himself of an exceptionally beautiful and ironic snort, puts on his hat and, with his prejudices girt about him like so many butcher knives, goes to see this production of "Hamlet" in the modern style.

What the critic, once he is in the theatre, sees is something that makes him feel, he confesses, rather like an ass. What he sees, for all his logical and sound prejudices, is a "Hamlet" actually more interesting, more exciting, more moving and more vivid than any "Hamlet" of other days his eyes have rested upon. His prejudices against the whole idea are still intact, but the damned thing convinces him against himself. He balks; he protests; he argues with himself. This is all nonsensical; this is production stuff for the groundlings; there is little critical justification for such whim-wham; it is all a practical joke. But to no avail. His logic can't resist him; the play gets him, as the popular phrase goes, and that's all there is to it. What seemed to him in advance

to be a mere charlatan's trick, a feat in faking,
now somehow seems nothing of the kind. Instead of disturbing the text, the production actually coddles it into renewed life. Instead of
being mere coggery to fetch the boobs, it actually
fetches the critic along with the rest. But maybe,
says the critic, somewhat in alarm, maybe I too
am one of these boobs; maybe two decades of association with bonehead audiences have reduced
me to their level; maybe I am being quietly taken
in along with all the others.

But the critic then proceeds to take stock of this
disturbing reflection. Is the presentation of "Hamlet" in modern habiliments and with modern stage
embellishments quite the absurd thing he has antecedently figured out to his complete satisfaction? It would begin to seem to the critic that
it wasn't. He reflects, for example, that the persons who most loudly hiccup at such a presentation are the same ones who are in the habit of
swallowing whole forty-five-year-old Juliets and
Ophelias, Mark Antonys who would obviously need
a Steinach operation before they would be able
to so much as kiss Cleopatra, Moorish Othellos
with Bloomsbury accents, Ariels with still visible
garter marks on their spirit legs, Falstaffs with
sofa-pillows passing for paunches, Dromio Robsons and Cranes who look no more alike than

Robsons and Cranes, Titanias with marcelled hair and ankles like beer-kegs, catarrhal Violas, Anglo-Saxon Illyrian dukes, two-hundred-pound Cassiuses, Macbeths with St. Louis haircuts and Romeos with their cheeks rouged and their eyelashes mascaroed like chorus men. He reflects further that those who, like himself, deride such a presentation are the same persons who willingly accept as proper Hauptmann's Silesian peasants speaking English, D'Annunzioan Giocondas sniffing American Beauty roses, and Shakespeare's Elizabethan stage itself converted into an elaborate Edison-lighted, Berlin-mechanized theatrical factory. If the conventional "Hamlet" costumed by the Eaves Costume Company is not laughable, why should one costumed by the Stein-Bloch Company be so inordinately comic? The critic hitches back his trousers to where they were in the first place, and dubiously scratches his head.

Other meditations now assail him. He reconsiders his prejudices. He begins to speculate that, if it is all right to play "Hamlet" against backgrounds by modern scene painters, as "Hamlet" is regularly played, why shouldn't it be equally all right to play it against modern tailors? If the one is meet, why isn't the other? He begins to argue with his prejudices that if it is absurd to picture a figure out of Danish saga in modern

dress, why isn't the conventional theatrical practice of picturing a figure out of Greek saga in
what, for all their ancient suggestion, are obviously
modern wigs, fleshings and sandals just as absurd.
For the critic recalls that Carlyle's doctrine of the
remission of judgment should hold as good in the
one case as in the other. Again, the critic goes
back to his prejudice as to the timelessness and
universality of "Hamlet" and his antecedent ironic
inquiry as to the justice of seeking to emphasize
these qualities by ridding the exhibition of its accustomed trappings. The critic at this point re-
minds himself that his objections would be well
taken were "Hamlet" a so-called realistic play,
but since "Hamlet" is nothing of the sort, since
it is rather the wild fancy of a great poetic imagination, it can matter no more how it be dressed
than it can matter how some such other beautiful
fairy tale out of more modern Danish fireside saga
as one of Hans Christian Andersen's be dressed.
Still further, the critic begins to remember that
it is a work of dramatic literary art that he is
dealing with, not merely a work of theatrical art,
and that nothing the theatre can do to a work of
dramatic literary art can change it much the one
way or the other. "Hamlet" remains "Hamlet,"
however it be played. It is part of the dramatic

imagination of every cultured man. The plays of hacks must be played according to definite, fixed standards; the plays of genius may be played in almost any manner. They survive out of their very deathlessness. Playing "Hamlet" in the dress and manner of today is quite as justifiable as playing a primitive folk song with a full modern orchestra.

The theatrical difficulty with "Hamlet," however, lies not so much in its dressing as in its direction. "Hamlet" is generally not only dressed in the Sixteenth Century manner, it is generally directed in the same manner. The stage decoration, the lighting and the other externals may be filtered through the improvements of modern stagecraft, but the direction of the text is uniformly as old-fashioned and as little cognizant of modern intelligence as that of a road production of "Uncle Tom's Cabin." The average Hamlet that we get is clothed in doublet and hose not only physically but mentally. The medallion about his neck contains the photograph of Augustin Daly's grandfather. Tradition is valuable to a family, a nation or a dog, but it is of small value to drama. I wasn't present at the first production of "Œdipus" in Athens, but I have strong doubts that it was one-tenth so good as even that which Martin

Harvey gave us a short time ago in the theatre at Sixty-second Street and Central Park West, New York.

The theory, however, that the universality and timelessness of "Hamlet" may be indicated by dressing it in modern clothes is at best a timid and weak-hearted stratagem. There is only one way to indicate and emphasize the universality and the timelessness of this or any other drama like it, and that is to play it without any clothes at all. You cannot make a play universal by dressing its characters after the manner of a single period and a single nation; you cannot make a play about a Dane of dim centuries universal by getting up the Dane like a modern Englishman or American; but you can make it universal and timeless by dressing it as men and women were dressed before universality and time were ever thought of, which is to say, as Adam and Eve dressed. I therefore propose the one and only true "Hamlet." I therefore propose a "Hamlet" stark naked.

THE PLAY AND THE PLAYWRIGHT

§ 1

It appears to be the belief of certain of our playwrights that the best way to create an authentic dramatic character is to take one of the conventional puppets of the stage and simply cause it to act in a manner opposite to that in which it customarily acts. Thus, in one of these playwrights' exhibits, the husband who finds that his wife has deceived him, instead of driving her into the night, lets out a yell of joy and presents her with a diamond necklace; the villain who pursues the proud beauty, instead of being thrown off the Brooklyn Bridge by the hero and his tried and true aide, the wily Hop Lee, successfully persuades her to succumb to his importunities; and the Prince weds Cinderella's step-sister. Authentic character, however, is unfortunately not to be negotiated in this wise. And while these playwright's naïve stratagem has, of course, succeeded in deceiving a number of gentlemen who write about the drama, it fails to satisfy a considerable number of others

173

that it is anything but an arbitrary and transparent trick.

Sound character is the drama's most difficult achievement. It is not to be achieved, as the playwrights in question seem to imagine, simply by bringing out onto the stage a George Broadhurst or an Augustus Thomas character and having it make a face at Mr. Broadhurst or Mr. Thomas. Such a character, may, true enough, be amusing in a freak way, as a man standing on his head and giving a eulogistic lecture on a new brand of footease is amusing, but it is hardly convincing. The auditor is constantly aware of the author's strain; he feels constantly that the character, for all its superficial integrity, is at bottom merely the stereotyped dramatic dummy with its coat turned inside out and its voice the voice of a clever ventriloquist hidden under the sofa. After all, for all the Jerome K. Jeromes, the Karl Ettlingers and the other deft lampooners of dramatic characters, the so-called manikins of the stage are often of the essence of actuality. We may smirk all we want to, but it remains that the world has more Hazel Kirkes, Squire Bartletts and Little Evas in it than Fanny Hawthornes, Captain Brassbounds and Duchesses de Nievres. One can't convert Little Eva into a more life-like and authentic character by the hocus-pocus of having her wink covertly at

Simon Legree behind Uncle's back and endorse the Jim Crow car, nor can one make Squire Bartlett more real than he is by having him whisper to La Moore that it is all quite all right so far as he is concerned and that he'll meet her for lunch at the Colony restaurant. Many of our playwrights, however, believe the contrary. And the practice of their belief results in the kind of dramatic characters that currently pass for forthright, honest and untheatrical depictions of *Homo sapiens,* but that are actually little more than the old stage marionettes who have been taken on a trip to visit Mrs. Horniman, who have had their hair cut by Bernard Shaw's barber, and who have come back home loudly contending that the world is flat, that the sun shines brightest at night, and that you can get excellent Scotch in New York at ten dollars a case.

§ 2

Of the hundreds of military plays that I have seen in the last twenty-five years, all but a few have had to do with adultery and seduction. Just why it is that the average dramatist can think of a soldier only as a guinea pig, I don't know, but the fact remains that the moment a playwright dresses up an actor in a military uniform all that he can

think up for him to do is either to get drunk and
chase the Colonel's wife around the table or ruin
a French peasant girl under promise of marriage.
The army of every nation is viewed by the playwrights of the respective nations as a large bachelor apartment. To listen to these playwrights,
one would be led to believe that being a soldier
was something like being the leading character in
an endless succession of Sacha Guitry plays. For
the soldiers in these military flummeries are merely
libidinous French actors given to pretending that
they are soldiers by the simple expedient of making their voices sound gruff and periodically pulling off their gloves as if they were very mad about
something.

§ 3

Contrary to what seems to be the general opinion
of me as a commentator on the drama, I have no
prejudice against sentiment; some of the very best
plays I know of are full of it from start to finish.
But the sentiment of these plays is based upon an
honest, cruel and very beautiful perception and
appreciation of human beings and of the grotesque
life they lead upon this funny sphere of ours.
The majority of American playwrights, however,
write what is merely actor-sentiment. It has no

relation to the minds and hearts of actual, living persons; it is simply a matter of actor speeches, grease-paint kisses and general idiocy. It is the species of sentiment that one gets from drug-store Christmas cards, moving picture sub-titles and fat women who have gone too far with the cocktail shaker. America is full of playwrights who believe that there is a definite consanguinity in romance and mental weakness, that romance finds its highest flower when the parties to it have the minds of half-wits and the emotions of pet kittens. And their plays, as a result, are romantic chiefly only to dramatic critics with the outlook of actors and other such males who wear lace on their cerebral pants. Women, I believe, are generally very much less susceptible to such exhibits than men. That is, on the average. There was a time, of course, when the so-called three-handkerchief play was certain to crowd the theatre at the matinée, but, with minor exception, that type of play no longer fetches the girls. As men have lost humor theatrically, women have gained it. And today the only forthright sentimental play that engages their interest is the one in which sentiment is concealed under thick layers of sex. The audience of women who used to snuffle over "East Lynne" and, later, over "Madame X," has practically disappeared. That audience today demands that its heart in-

terest be below the waistline. That audience
wants its sentiment in pink pajamas and a green
hat.

§ 4

Ashley Dukes has said of Wedekind that as a
dramatist he is something more than an eccentric,
but something less than a creative genius. In the
celebrated "Erdgeist," the most typical of Wedekind's plays, and one that may be taken in illus-
tration of his work as a whole, this eccentricity and
creative genius carry on a four act fight with the
honors even up to the last round and with eccentricity then scoring a clean knock-out. A drama of
very considerable ironic force up to that moment, the whole structure suddenly gives way and
collapses because of the weight of eccentricity that
Wedekind superimposes upon it. Eccentricity
may perhaps be not the exact term. Technical be-
fuddlement describes the cause of the *débâcle* more
aptly. The dramatist found the germ of the later
Expressionism lurking in his mind, but when he
tried to get the germ upon paper it turned out to
be a bubonic plague. He was so little the master
of the idea that dawned upon him that it eluded
his grasp completely and exaggerated itself so
absurdly that it turned upon itself as burlesque.

178

The result spells disaster to an important portion of his drama.

Being half-genius and half-mountebank, Wedekind is able to scale but half way up the side of the mountainous themes he has chosen for himself. He gets half way up to the top, to the huzzas of the crowd, and then slides comically down to the bottom again on his seat. The line between profound tragedy and ribald humor is as thin as a hair. Only a full-blown genius can hold tragedy back from the sudden pitfall of mockery and laughter. Wedekind cannot. He moves up to the brink cautiously enough, but, just as one is beginning to feel that the danger is past, his foot slips and he lands ludicrously in the mud-pile. The trouble with him is not difficult to deduce. He seems never to be quite clear as to just what he is driving at. More than any other conspicuous dramatist of modern Europe, he is what his own people know as a *zusammensetzender Schauspieldichter*, which, in gin English, is a synthetic playwright. He is a compound of naturalist, symbolist, impressionist, expressionist, realist, satirist, idealist and mystic, with the graduation and adjustment far from perfect. And each of his plays such as "Erdgeist," "Die Büchse der Pandora," "Frühlings Erwachen" and "Oaha" thus comes to resemble a Siamese twin playing hide and seek

179

with itself. He is Strindberg one minute, Maeterlinck the next, Georg Kaiser the next and Sudermann, Shaw and Gorki rolled into one a minute later, with the spook of Nietzsche constantly tickling his ear with a feather.

As is often the way with criticism, however, once it has blandly ticked off a dramatist and exposed his inadequacies, it has to confess (to itself, if not publicly) that for all it so sagaciously has found wrong with him he yet remains a vital and moving theatrical force. Such a vital and moving force, genius or no genius, Wedekind is. That his talents have not been appreciated so greatly in England and America as on the Continent is easily explained. The reception of sniggers and snickers that greeted his "Erdgeist" in New York, for example, is illuminating in more ways than one. In the first place, the Anglo-Saxon theatregoer refuses to differentiate between laughter of one kind and another. Anything that makes him laugh, he promptly sets down and dismisses as generically comic. The volitional laughter that he vouchsafes a flying custard pie is the same to him as the involuntary laughter he vouchsafes a crescendo nervousness. Thus, when he finds himself laughing negatively to relieve the embarrassment of his too acute sensitiveness, he blames the drama-

tic scene for his own weakness. It is thus that
Wedekind fails in America just as, on a lower
level, the Grand Guignol thrillers fail. A second reason for the failure of such a play as "Erdgeist" lies in the disposition of the Anglo-Saxon
audience to view as comedy what the Continental
European views as drama. Thus when, in certain portions of Wedekind's play, such degenerate
hors d'œuvres as flagellation, Lesbianism and the
like are touched on, the Anglo-Saxon smiles where
the German, Frenchman or Italian wears a straight
and thoughtful face. A German audience will accept a nance and a Lesbian as dramatic characters;
an English or an American audience will only
guffaw at them. The study in degeneracy called
"Vatermord," which had all Berlin by the ears
several years ago, would be howled into the storehouse before Saturday night if it were to be produced in New York.

The American miscarriage of "Erdgeist" has
been erroneously, I believe, ascribed by the reviewers to the manner and method of its presentation. While it is true that Wedekind's fervent
dramatic manuscript was directed and acted as if
it were a menthol inhaler, I can't believe that it
would have prospered more greatly whatever the
nature of the direction and acting. The trouble

lies deeper than that. It lies in a dramatist whose mind is as alien to the American theatregoer as the mind of George Ade, say, is alien to the German. Wedekind is the most cruel and forthrightly devastating dramatic mind that the stage of our immediate day has known. It is his misfortune that his technical equipment is not up to the demands of that mind. He is therefore doomed to pass into dramatic history as a mere symptom of what might have been an important talent.

§ 5

In a comparatively young drama, like our American, the character of the villain is ever over-emphasized. It is only in more mature drama, which gains its maturity from an older culture, philosophy and civilization, that the force of evil is not arbitrarily heightened by way of achieving dramatic conflict easily and with a minimum of imaginative energy. The weaker the villain, the more difficult it is to project the drama implicit in the characters of the hero and heroine. Paint your villain in loud colors, and the job becomes relatively simple. Thus, melodrama is of all the dramatic forms the easiest, and high comedy the most difficult. For great tragedy is its own villain.

§ 6

In a day of quick-step dramaturgy, in a day
when a restless audience may be kept in its seats
only by drama that either shoots off a revolver
every fifteen minutes or has its heroine chased up
and down the aisles by a gorilla, in such a day
the placid and leisurely play must have a hard
time of it. For the audience of to-day must have
its drama as it has its motor-cars: self-starting,
speedy, noisy—and just a bit smelly. A rapid-
fire story of a street-walker's ascension to pure
love, an emotions-pressed-while-you-wait tale of a
mother whose hop-head son takes her in *crim. con.*
with a gigolo, an eat-'em-alive yarn about a pale-
face who falls for a South Sea Island squaw—
such recherché manure is manna to that audience's
taste. But for the urbane and slow-moving drama,
however beautiful, the audience in point cares no
more than a Mexican does for bath salts.

§ 7

The common statement that a writer's style is
a true reflection of the man, that his style is an
outgrowth of his personality, is often absurd.
The truth is that, in the case of many a writer,
the personality is an outgrowth of the style. The

writer creates a fictitious picture of himself as man in his style and then takes color from his style by way of living up to the popular conception of him. Shaw is an excellent example. His style is of telegraphic dynamite all compact: mentally aphrodisiac adjectives, meat-eating verbs, sequences that are tipsy with the wine of gaiety. The man himself is intrinsically exactly the opposite. Shaw, the man, is no more the blood-brother of the Shaw style than Cabell, the man, is the blood-brother of the Cabell style. Shaw's style is less a true reflection of Shaw as man than, let us say, of John Maynard Keynes as man. Shaw, however, wise showman that he is, has simply created himself in its own image. He has carefully evolved a completely alien and artificial style, set it up as a dummy, and then appropriated the dummy's trousers for himself.

Dreiser's style is Dreiser; Lewis' style is Lewis; Harold Bell Wright's style is Wright. But Lardner's style is no more Lardner, *Homo sapiens* and Great Neck householder, than Dunsany's style is Dunsany, *Homo sapiens* and Gargantuan oyster eater. The ivory elephant that the estimable and realistic Lord wears on a black ribbon around his neck is a concession to his style, just as the open-collared shirt and tousled hair of Jack London were

184

a concession to his. Style is less often the man than the concept of him he wishes his readers to have. The sentence structure, the sequences, the juxtapositions and the verbal trickeries and cadences of many men of letters are no more reflections of their inner beings than the rôles most actors play are reflections of theirs.

§ 8

A so-called dream play is one in which the hero or heroine goes to sleep at the end of the first act and in which the audience generally beats the hero or heroine to it by from ten to fifteen minutes. This somnolence is induced by the long and tedious preparation that is usually necessary for the dream part of the drama. It takes a playwright up to half past nine to introduce, one after the other, the various persons, properties and events which are to figure in the ensuing dream and by the time the introductions are accomplished everyone is pretty well tuckered out.

Dream plays are of three kinds. There is the dream play in which the hero goes to sleep and dreams that he is living in the age of William the Conqueror and that the heroine is the fair Gismonda held captive by the dastardly knight, Eric the Saw-toothed. Then there is the dream play in which the hero takes an overdose of toddy and dreams that he is dreaming a dream in which he dreams that the treasure chest for which all the characters have been looking in Act I is hidden in the old oak tree on Squire Meyerbeer's estate, said treasure chest being duly found there when he wakes up with a serio-comic hangover in the last act. And finally there is the dream play in which the hero, beset by troubles, takes a snooze and dreams a dream in which all the characters who have caused the troubles figure grotesquely. The chief fault with most of these dream plays lies in their dream portions. A dream should move with the ease and fluidity of rushing water or curling smoke. But on the stage a dream usually moves with the ease and fluidity of a Coney Island sight-seeing bus. The average dream that we see worked out on the stage is like nothing so much as the big battle scene in "The Soudan." Not only do the stagehands make a terrible racket shifting the numerous scenes and properties, not only do the bunchlights and spotlights add to the hullaballoo with a wealth of sizzling, and not only do the actors stumble noisily over chairs and tables in the dark, but, to boot, some one is always kicking his foot through the scrim fore-curtain or chasing his hat which has fallen into the footlight trough. I am pretty good at working up illusion for myself—I once even succeeded in getting myself to believe dramatically that Edmund Breese was a man before the power of whose remarkable mind everyone trembled—but I'll be hanged if I can get myself to view as part of a dream a scene in which several stagehands in Kuppenheimer suits and Truly Warner derbies, and chewing tobacco, are clearly to be seen monkeying with the guide-ropes.

§ 9

Not many playwrights have given us more pleasure in the theatre than Schnitzler, but it has been the gay-sad Schnitzler of "Anatol" and "Lie-belei," "Reigen" and the "Komtesse Mizzi," not the Viennese Brieux of "Der Einsame Weg" and "Der Ruf des Lebens," "Das Vermächtnis" and "Professor Bernhardi," who has given it. In his best plays, Schnitzler has dramatized the philosophy of emotion; in his worst, the emotion that proceeds from philosophy. A dramatization of the latter, unfortunately, never rings quite true in the theatre, for the simple reason, perhaps, that, so far as drama goes, it puts the cart before the horse and for the further simple reason that when you put the cart before the horse on the stage, you may achieve satire or burlesque, but not forth-right, moving drama. It has been such drama that Schnitzler has aimed for in these theatrically less effective of his plays, and he has missed it. The field of the straight-faced so-called problem play, the play of argument and deduction, is not the field of Schnitzler. His field lies over the way where the moonlight of yesterday still silvers forgotten flowers, where love never thinks, and where the axis of the earth is Cupid's arrow. From that field he has brought forth a tender love-liness such as few modern dramatists have, but wandering from that field all that he has garnered is an inferior grade of French drama.

Schnitzler is at his best when he writes with a pen dipped into evanescent Tokay, when his desk lamp is a delicate pink electrolier, and when the hurdy-gurdy under his window is playing "Rosen aus dem Süden." That is the Schnitzler of plays that have been at once the charm and delight of the modern theatre. He is at his worst when he writes with a pen dipped into indelible ink, when the hard daylight streams through his window, and when the hurdy-gurdy has gone on its way. That is the Schnitzler of plays that ape profundity and that, whether consciously or not, seek to conceal a platitudinous philosophy and palm it off as some-thing extraordinary by the obvious dodge of an-

nouncing it through the mouth of the leading character and causing all the secondary characters to
stand aghast at it. Nowhere are the unfortunate
results of Schnitzler's excursion from his true
medium so clearly to be observed as in such of his
plays as "Das Vermächtnis" and "Der Ruf des
Lebens." In the present-day theatre, if not in the
library, they skirt perilously the coasts of travesty.
The most skilful stage direction cannot entirely
safeguard them from a modern audience's recalci-
trant humors. Their windy philosophy of life
and sex is theatrically as out of date as gas footlights and their dolours over what has ceased to
make audiences sniffle since the women's clubs
gave up Sudermann and since Pinero was knighted
have the ring of someone weeping lustily because
Chester A. Arthur is dead.

One fears, indeed, that the day of lengthy
philosophizing over sex is done in the theatre. To
interest a reputable audience in the modern theatre,
sex may be treated only comically or romantically.
For less reputable but even more profitable audiences, it may be treated smuttily, but for the
kind of audiences the better-grade theatre caters
to it may be handled only in terms of clowning on
the one hand or moonlit gondolas on the other.
The modern audience, cultured or not cultured,
wants its sex without too much talk; it demands,

in a manner of speaking, at least one seduction to
every ten sides of dialogue. In addition, the
Schnitzler attitude toward sex as disclosed in the
plays under discussion is an attitude that has gone
out of dramatic fashion. It belongs to the theatrical day when every female character who had
lost her virginity promptly went upstairs and put
on a black dress. The drama of yesterday constantly belied life in associating adultery inevitably
with melancholia: the heroines of yesterday were
made by their authors regularly to confound sexual gratification with spiritual depression. This
dramatic attitude toward violations of Numero
Sette has plainly undergone a philosophic earthquake since the Nineties, with the result that any
heroine who would today have the audacity to
come into the front parlor and let out a bawl
because she had succumbed to the plausible charms
of a lieutenant in the Coldstream Guards or the
family osteopath would be greeted with a very fine
assortment of cat-calls.

The philosophy of such a play as "Der Ruf des
Lebens," penetrating its bog of verbiage, amounts,
so far as I can make out, simply to this: it is better
to be alive than dead. As a piece of philosophy,
I am ready to grant that there is something in what
Dr. Schnitzler says, but I object to staying up
until eleven o'clock at night to hear him say it.

§ 10

We read frequently in the critical prints of the sophisticated melodrama. What is a sophisticated melodrama? A sophisticated melodrama, I take it, is one in which the characters never get excited about the things which characters in unsophisticated melodrama get excited about. In the ordinary melodrama, when the hero is tied and gagged by the villain and strapped to the railroad track, he gets slightly angry about it. But not so in sophisticated melodrama. He merely suggests that the villain exercise the precaution not to break the cigars in his breast pocket, quietly quotes a phrase or two from Dante Gabriel Rossetti, and lets it go at that. In sophisticated melodrama, the "Unhand me, dog!" of unsophisticated melodrama is converted into an epigram, whiskey and soda are substituted for revolvers, and the scene is transfered from the East River wharf at midnight to a Park Avenue apartment. The characters never run to the exits, but walk. In addition, instead of shouting, they lower their voices so that everyone back of the sixth row has to use an ear-trumpet; and, instead of disparaging the villain every time he leaves the stage, they remark that he isn't such a bad fellow at heart after all.

§ 11

What was left over of the preposterous kicking
and braying that were indulged in by Israel Zangwill while he was last in the United States has
been incorporated by him into the dramatic form
and given the name "We Moderns." With a rapid
percussion of miff and grumble, sulk and spleen,
huff and belly-ache, the M. Zangwill, who talks
like a blackball, gets up on his hind legs and opens
his mouth wide on the novel subject of the Younger
Generation. Doubtless under the belief that no
one has thus far ever thought to point out certain weaknesses of the present Younger Generation,
and jumping at the subject in high glee, he goes
through the stale rigmarole with a perfectly
straight face—always excepting the nose—and suc-
ceeds admirably, after three hours of indignant
yowling and yammering, in saying less, and saying
it more idiotically, than the youngest Princeton or
Yale author who has written on the theme. The
play is a stilted, affected, and thoroughly ridiculous
piece of bombast. The characters representing the
current young of the species no more resemble actual human beings than do the Yellow Kid, Pore
Li'l Mose, or the Enfants Katzenjammer. Zangwill's modern flapper, for example, though a
cigarette-smoking, cocktail-drinking, wise-cracking

cutie who frequents loose studio parties and the like, has her own night key and is up on the latest international Greenwich Village literature, is yet completely ignorant of sex, still imagines that babies are brought by the *Ephippiorhynchus senegalensis,* and believes that a kiss on the lips signifies physical defloration. I am not trying to be funny; I set down the literal fact. The other representatives of the Younger Generation are scarcely less piquant. They have illegitimate babies, climb down water-spouts and show their legs to enthusiastic crowds of onlookers, pose in the nude, take up the family servants as boon companions, make rendezvous with professional seducers in their own drawing-rooms, and never lie down without perching their feet on the tops of the couches. They also quote poetry on every possible occasion and tell their parents to go to hell. The net impression of all of which is of the Messrs. Scott Fitzgerald and Stephen Vincent Benét, both beautifully boozy, rolling downstairs with their arms around each other. There are bad plays that are simply bad plays, and there are bad plays that, in addition to being bad, are irritating in their irascibility and contentiousness. "We Moderns" is in the latter category. Zangwill's indignation, which appears to embrace everything that Hilaire Belloc hasn't yet thought of and which, in its American manifestations, covered everything from the Pennsylvania Railroad's habit of locking up the *cabinets d'aisances* while the train is passing through Elizabeth, N. J., to Otto Kahn's failure to send him the right kind of cigars —this wholesale indignation is spread over the play like so much sour dough.

§ 12

In the drama of the Nineties, whenever a hero in the throes of despair lifted his eyes tc heaven and said, "Oh God—if there be one—help me!", a bolt of lightning promptly obliged him and laid the villain low. In the drama of more recent years, however, what usually follows the appeal is two hours of ostensibly consoling Swedenborgian philosophy, presumably inculcated in the beseecher's mind by the Providence addressed.

§ 13

The Hungarian manuscript market being pretty well exhausted in the matter of quality, at least for the time being, the American theatrical impresario is currently deluding himself into buying Magyar gold-bricks under the impression that they are masterpieces. Up to relatively recent

years, our producers knew Budapest only as a
place from which the Café Boulevard and Little
Hungary restaurant recruited red-coated fiddlers.
All that some of us could do to persuade them that
there were other things in the city on the Danube
than rackety gipsy orchestras, beribboned tam-
bourine pounders and willing blonde chamber-
maids went for nothing. We were put down as
so many Aubrey Pipers who were dredging up a
lot of queer-sounding names that no one had ever
heard of before simply by way of showing off the
cosmopolitan result of having spent a week or
two of a Summer vacation in Central Europe.
And then—some time later—a couple of the local
producers simultaneously got hold of the manuscript of one of the poorest of the modern Hungarian plays and ran a race to see who could first
get it on. This play, which consisted in essence
merely of a commonplace London drawing-room
comedy with the Charles Hawtrey of the occasion
dressed up in a swallowtail with a red satin lin-
ing and with his eyebrows penciled upward at an
angle of forty-five degrees, stampeded the rest
of the managers. The astounding novelty of it
sent them packing to the cable offices and shortly
thereafter the ships bound westward were laden
with countless Hungarian manuscripts which might
have been bought a few years earlier for United

Cigar Store coupons but which now called for prices so fancy that it was not long before Kuhn, Loeb and Company had to angel one of the largest producing firms to enable it to buy even the prologue of a three-act play.

Among these manuscripts that were brought over there were, as some of us had been reporting for a number of years, a half dozen or so of very considerable beauty and merit—and also, as we had reported, many more that were of the second, third and fourth rank. But the boom was on and up and down Broadway and in the catalogues of the publishers such names as Imre, Ferenz, Lászlo and Melchior crowded out the erstwhile Augustuses, Owens, Juleses and Samuels. The good plays and the poor ones were swallowed as one, not only by the producers, but by the public, and not only by the public, but by the critics. Molnár became the patron saint of the Rialto, and Dregely, Vajdá, Pasztór, Lengyel, Biró and their Budapest brothers began to buy silk pajamas and Fords. The Sunday newspapers, that had for twenty years been devoting their theatrical pages to stories telling how Maude Adams had been carried on the stage by her mother at the age of two sucking a milk bottle, how Sidney Rosenfeld had got the idea for one of his masterworks while listening to a German brass band playing Chopin's Étude in Thirds, and how the scholarly Richard Mansfield invariably recited "Cancionero" in its entirety while he shaved before the mirror in his private car, now went in front and bustle for articles indiscriminately hailing the genius of any playwright whose name had accents on letters not accented in the French and whose plays consisted of a Schnitzlerian sentimental philosophy removed from the customary scene in a middle-class living-room or an artist's studio and placed in a scene representing either a railroad culvert or an antechamber to the celestial regions. And the professional critics, who hitherto had fought tooth and nail to keep the American stage free from foreign contamination and alien sex evils and safe, thank God!, for uplifting *Festspiele* in which life-long cripples were cured by reciting the Ten Commandments and in which the divorce question was settled by a child's critical illness—these professional critics now tripped over themselves in lifting up their hallelujas to any dramatist whose name would give S. Stanwood Menken a patriotic colic and whose plays allowed that adultery might on occasion be something other than what Alfred McCann wrote about.

This Hungarian wayzgoose has been one of the chief sources of amusement to gourmets of the *délicat* in affairs theatrical. Some fine and dignified plays have come out of it, as they know; and so have many more that have been no whit better than the average American play of commerce. But the whale-oil has been smeared upon them all, whether good or bad. That is, until very recently. As is ever the case, when worms turn, they somersault. There is no well-considered gyration in such cases; what ensues is a wild flip-flop. And so we now engage a vast nose-fingering, as indiscriminate and as addle-pated as the antecedent eulogies.

§ 14

Galsworthy, who never writes badly, often thinks badly. Not as a novelist, true enough, but as a dramatist. It is his general plan to posture a profound thesis and gradually think it out of an audience's consciousness with deceptive theatrical shifts. He puts on his shining suit of armor, sharpens his lance on the sole of his boot, jumps astride his breathless charger and then dashes full tilt into a trick mirror. He sees his thesis clearly enough from a distance, but it blurs somewhat grotesquely on him as he nears it. He aims bravely at von Hindenburg and brings down George Sylvester Viereck. Yet he is usually a sufficiently talented craftsman to deceive many of his auditors.

He can cover up banality so dexterously with good writing that by the time his audience has got the sand out of its eyes the play is already over and it doesn't know whether it was bamboozled or not.

§ 15

A Few Footnotes on O'Neill.—The dramatic technic of Eugene O'Neill consists in the filtering of an ironic vision of humanity through a sieve of pitiful despair and the embellishment of the residuum with the species of ejaculation customarily associated with longshoremen and vice-presidents of the United States.

(b)

O'Neill has a lot to answer for. Before he came upon the scene, most of our younger playwrights were content simply to write bad plays and let it go at that. But no sooner did he appear than most of these playwrights began to try to write good plays of the kind he was writing and to turn out even worse ones than they had turned out before. For the only things that they had in common with O'Neill were cuss words. Yet they believed that, though they lacked the latter's measure of genius, they could write the species of drama that he wrote with one hand tied behind their backs. All that was necessary to achieve an O'Neill play, they imagined, was to take a Gorki play, dress up all the characters as either sailors or farmers, cut out the one faintly humorous line in the second act, and then cause the characters to call one another obscene names at intervals of every few minutes. What resulted, you know. The American stage began to disclose an assortment of plays that, aside from some loud oaths and a final scene in which a sea captain or a New England farmer went crazy, resembled the O'Neill drama just about as closely as a marinierte herring resembles Mozart's quartet in E flat major.

(c)

Before the advent of O'Neill, the young American playwright was busy writing plays in which an attempt was made to capture a drawing-room atmosphere by the employment of such locutions as "Pray inform Senator Murphy that the verisimilitude is distinctly rococo"; today, the young American playwright is busy writing plays that try to capture a water-front atmosphere by having all the characters periodically call each other a lousy cockroach.

(d)

O'Neill is frequently found to be an advocate and practitioner of the dramatic intensification method of Strindberg. Emotions and actions are from moment to moment crowded together by him and piled atop one another into a series of constant explosions. It is a method full of danger to the playwright, as there is always the difficulty in keeping this side of the hair-line that separates and distinguishes intensification from mere bald overemphasis and exaggeration. O'Neill is not always successful in differentiating between the two, and the result, when he becomes confused, runs his drama perilously near the rocks of anamorphosis.

(e)

Among the criticisms of "The Fountain," I note a dissatisfaction with the American Indian as O'Neill has presented him. O'Neill has seen fit to give his Indians a measure of intelligible discourse. This has come as a great shock to those of my colleagues who, since their Edward S. Ellis and "The Girl I Left Behind Me" days, have been firmly convinced that the only things American Indians were capable of saying to one another

were either "Ugh!" or "Big Chief Walla-Walla
has spoken!"

(f)

It is amusing to look back upon the emission of
drool precipitated by the presentation of O'Neill's
"All God's Chillun Got Wings." Participants in
the geyser of nonsense included everyone from
Prof. Dr. Arthur Brisbane, of the Bibliothèque
Hearst, to Colonel Billy Mayfield, of the Benev-
olent Protective Order of the Ku Klux Klan,
Texas Lodge, from the dramatic critic of the
Windgap, Pa., *International News-Herald* to the
shepherd of the Baptist flock at Horsecough, Va.,
and from a member of the faculty of Princeton
University to the owners, publishers, editors, and
editorial writers of half the Southern newspapers.
Black men protested in the press that the play was
a libel on their race, since it showed an educated
Negro taking for wife a drab of the streets. White
men protested in turn that it was an insult to their
race, since it showed a white woman, no matter
what her morals, taking unto her bosom a coon.
The heroic Colonel Mayfield, in an editorial in
the *Fiery Cross*, demanded the immediate dispatch
of the author on the ground that he was a Catholic
and hence was doubtless trying to stir up the

Negroes to arm, march on Washington, and burn
down the Nordic White House. The always pas-
sionately sincere Brisbane, in an editorial in the
Hearst journals, cried Look Out! There Will Be
Race Riots! The New York moralmorons were
hot with indignation because O'Neill showed a
white woman kissing a Negro's hand. Dramatic
critics denounced the play vehemently on the
ground that it was played by a real Negro and a
white actress, which was awful. The American
Legion, through certain of its mediums of expression published in the Middle West, announced flam-
ingly that it considered the play subversive of 100
per cent American patriotism in that it sought to
undo all the good that was accomplished by the
Legion's winning of the late war. The lucid argument of the Legion was that a piece of writing that
dealt with miscegenation and that was supposed to
be authentically American was sure to alienate certain of our late allies in arms. It was the further
belief of the Legion's spokesmen in the Middle West
that there was German propaganda concealed in the
enterprise. In all probability, observed the Legion's spokesmen, the producers of the play would
be found to be either German or of German descent. The names of these producers, whom the
Texas Chapter of the Ku Klux on the other hand
insisted must be Jews, were clearly of a German-

Yiddish flavor, to wit, Macgowan, O'Neill and Jones.

It has been some time since a play has succeeded in causing so much commotion. Why this particular play caused it, I can't make out, unless it is that the number of half-wits in America is increasing much faster than any of us has believed. There is absolutely nothing in the play that is in the slightest degree offensive to any human being above the mental level of a dog-show judge. The initial thread of theme is simply "Abie's Irish Rose" with Abie blacked up. And the final turn of theme is simply that of Wilson Barrett's "The Sign of the Cross" with the off-stage howling of lions left out. "Uncle Tom's Cabin" has been played at different times by six companies with real Negroes in the rôle of Uncle Tom—two black prize-fighters (the famous Peter Jackson was one of them) are among those who have played the part—and no one, even south of the Mason-Dixon line, has so much as let out a whisper when these real Negroes have fondled and kissed the white Little Evas. The late Bert Williams not only played in many sketches with white women, but cavorted gayly for years with white feminine flesh on our music show stage. And Belasco has lately and popularly in "Lulu Belle" mixed up blacks and whites indiscriminately. In

"All God's Chillun Got Wings," there is no physical contact between the Negro and the white woman save in the matter of their hands. Once, true enough, after a scene of frenzied mental aberration, the white actress is called upon to kiss the Negro's hands "as a child might, tenderly and gratefully," but the intrinsic feeling and impression here are not far removed from the Uncle Tom-Little Eva kind of thing.

To object to the play because it treats of miscegenation is to object to the drama "Othello" ("Othello is made by Shakespeare in every respect a Negro"—August Wilhelm Schlegel), or to the opera "L'Africaine," or to the Kipling story of "Georgie Porgie." To object to it because it shows a man and a woman of different color and of antagonistic race in the attitude of lovers is to object to Sheldon's "The Nigger," De Mille's "Strongheart," Selwyn's "The Arab" and the lately produced "White Cargo," to mention but four out of any number of popular theatre plays that have gone their way unmolested, to say nothing of "Madame Butterfly," "Lakmé" and "Aïda." To argue against it that, since it shows a white woman marrying a Negro, it therefore *ipso facto* places its mark of approval on such marriages is to argue that since "Tosca" shows a woman stabbing a chief of police to death it therefore *ipso facto* places its mark of approval on the universal murdering of policemen. The O'Neill play, it is quite true, shows a certain white woman and a certain Negro in the married relation, but it obviously has no more intention of generalizing from this single and isolated case than such a play as "The Bowery After Dark" which, following the line of profound logic that has been exercised in the case of the O'Neill play, would seek to prove that all Chinamen are bent upon getting white women into dark cellars for purposes of anatomical dirty work. "All God's Chillun Got Wings" is simply O'Neill's attempt to show what *would* happen psychologically *if* a white woman, whatever her station, *were* to marry a Negro. Plainly enough, in order to show what *would* happen, he has theatrically and dramatically to deduce his findings from the visualized situation. Otherwise, save he wished to resort to the bogus dream formula—which doubtless would have pacified the dolts who were so much worked up—he would have no play. How far he has succeeded in achieving his intention, the readers of the play may judge for themselves. It is my own belief that he has achieved the end he had in view. His play is unquestionably enfeebled by its sketchiness, by its perhaps too great economy of means, but it nonetheless presents its theme sincerely, intelligently,

206

sympathetically and, it seems to me, dramatically. There is a measure of cloudiness in its final passages, yet this cloudiness is doubtless inherent in the very nature of the theme. The hoopdedoodle that was raised over that theme and over the theatrical presentation of the play expounding it must make any half-way intelligent Pullman porter shake his head sadly in pity for the mentality of a certain portion of the race that, by the grace of God, sits in the plush chairs.

§ 16

By the simple trick of writing an ordinary French boulevard farce-comedy and naming the characters Benvenuto Cellini, the Duke of Florence and the like, a playwright sometimes manages to produce a divertissement with a doubly comic edge, for what might not be funny in the instance of a character named Raoul Duval becomes peculiarly humorous when that character, without changing the lines or situations in the slightest, is named Cellini. The device is exactly akin to the old burlesque show dodge which consisted in loudly heralding the entrance of George Washington, sounding the trumpets, and then having the German comedian come on. The Cellini in point is no more Cellini than he is Amerigo Vespucci, but it doesn't matter in the least. It is the grotesque idea that he is the estimable Benvenuto that produces the laughs. The stratagem recalls to me a favorite diversion of my college days. In that innocent and juvenile period I used to derive some pleasure from fashioning burlesque shows by the simple device of taking a script like "The Lady of Lyons," say, and, keeping it intact, merely changing the names of the characters from Claude Melnotte, Colonel Damas and Pauline Deschappelles to Grover Cleveland, Doctor Munyon and Lillian Russell, or one like "East Lynne" and changing Sir Francis Levison, Archibald Carlyle and Lady Isabel to Stonewall Jackson, Adlai E. Stevenson and Josie Mansfield.

§ 17

The American commercial manager does not hold to the opinion that plays aren't written but rewritten; he holds to the opinion that plays aren't rewritten but refurnished. No matter what the scene is in the original draft of a play, this manager forthwith takes out all the furniture and moves in a bed. His theory seems to be that the surest way to get audiences into a theatre is to fit up the stage with a five thousand dollar bedroom set and incorporate in it a ten-cent dramatization of the old some-say-she-do-and-some-say-she-don't smoking-car story.

§ 18

The charm of the Continental, as opposed to the Anglo-Saxon, comedy of sex is that it deals frankly and realistically with adultery instead of trying to persuade its audiences that every time a man and a woman are on the point of the sexual act they are forestalled by the ringing of the telephone or by a knock on the door or by a fat comedian who has been hiding under the bed. The majority of Anglo-Saxon reviewers, who echo the prejudices of their readers—both naturally and because they do not wish to take chances offending what is called the home circulation—object to such a treatment of sex. They will laugh at and endorse sex treated farcically or in terms of comedy only when, as I have observed, it is opportunely interrupted by the telephone bell, the knock on the door, or the periodic and disturbing entrance of Marcel, the French waiter. This satisfies their sense of morality. No commandment is violated. But the moment a telephone doesn't ring or a knock doesn't come to save the situation, their

generic morality is offended and, however much
they may laugh, they yet realize that they have a
duty to perform for their readers. If there has
ever been shown in New York a farce or a comedy
in which adultery has been realized and which has
received good notices from the gentlemen on the
papers, I do not know its name. The good notices are reserved for the "Fair and Warmers," the
"Twin Beds" and other such pieces in which
adultery is only toyed with. To get by the American reviewer, a sex farce or comedy must be
merely a teaser.

§ 19

Many things that a German audience takes
seriously, an American audience regards merely
as food for snickers. In our theatre, for example, if the hero of a play kisses the heroine with
an unduly prolonged and adhesive smack, a liberal
portion of the customers constitute themselves
critics of the osculation by making noises suggestive of a wholesale sucking of horehound lozenges.
In Germany, on the other hand, a kiss lasting so
long that the audience has ample time during it to
consume at least two knackwurst sandwiches, a
box of sardellen and maybe three or four dill
pickles arouses not the slightest objection.

§ 20

A leading defect in some of the better American attempts at dramatic writing lies in the effort of the authors to broaden the aspect and importance of their themes by departing from the specific to the general. Not content with allowing their characters to tell their special stories, they periodically step to one side, pull a ruler out of their pockets, and indulge themselves in a blackboard lecture proving by statistics that there are thousands of persons in the world like their characters and that they are going through the same crises and vicissitudes. Nothing, of course, so weakens a drama as a sortie of this kind. A good dramatist never generalizes; he leaves generalization to his auditors. You cannot make "Way Down East" anything more than the balderdash it is by giving the Squire a five minute speech arguing that there are men all over the world who drive erring girls out into snowstorms.

§ 21

One has a feeling that, even if it be dexterously handled, the theme of non-resistance is not too well suited to drama. Non-resistance is itself palpably not dramatic; drama consists in resistance of one sort or another, physical or mental. When the protagonist of a play is an exponent of the doctrine of non-resistance and conducts himself accordingly, conflict, the chief essential of drama, must inevitably pale. The result is a play that devotes itself for the major portion to mere talk and, save the dramatist be a great wit, a philosopher or a great genius, the second result is tedium. Such a play as, say, Galsworthy's "A Bit o' Love" thus fails in much the same way and for much the same reason that such a one as Molnar's non-resistance play, "Fashions for Men," fails. The central characters in both are of a piece, and both playwrights, by virtue of the nature of the theme into which they have incorporated them, have been unsuccessful in dramatizing them. Like any other playwright, Galsworthy or Molnar has been most successful with the thematic doctrine of resistance. Non-resistance remains a theme for farce.

§ 22

In late years there has crept into the critical vocabulary, and caused considerable itching there, a shading of the word *sophisticated*. The term is generally employed in a slightly condescending and opprobrious sense. One takes it, in its critical color, to mean that the playwright so designated is a fellow made cynical by his cosmic experiences, one bored by everything that does not bore the normal human being, one who cannot see the beauty of the Alps for their chilblains, the romance of the desert for its pebbles in the shoe or the charm of pure love for its attendant conversation. In the case of the play thus dubbed, one is given to understand that, like its author, it mocks at the things in life held sacred by the majority of good folk. Yet, after due meditation of the subject, I come to the conclusion that what our critics usually call a sophisticated play is anything but what they seem to imagine it is; that it is, to the contrary, generally at bottom much less sophisticated, in the accepted meaning of the word, and much more ingenuous than the type of play they look upon as the reverse.

The so-called sophisticated play, estimating it from a survey of the list of exhibits that have been described with the adjective, is simply a play whose author idealizes in terms of disillusion what other dramatists idealize in terms of illusion. We have an excellent example in the case of Brieux's "Les Hannetons" on the one side and some such play as Henry Arthur Jones' "The Case of Rebellious Susan" on the other. The former postures two lovers who are not married and yet are inevitably and mercilessly drawn together after various difficulties; the latter, two lovers who are married and who are inevitably and ironically drawn together after various difficulties. The so-called sophisticated comedy is here surely, for all its surface aspect, the more profoundly sentimental of the two. And in the same way we discover that, for all their initial design of dramatic circumstance and occasional dialogue, most of the plays of this kind are fundamentally of a philosophy as guileless in its disillusion as that of the others is guileful in its illusion.

Since the adjective is for the most part assigned to plays that deal in one way or another with sex, a contemplation of the manner in which they approach and handle the subject will clearly disclose the essential nature of such plays. As an example of the so-called sophisticated sex play, we may take one of Schnitzler's; as an example of what may be called the unsophisticated sex play, we may take one of Anzengruber's. I deliberately choose examples that apparently make the contention difficult of proof. Yet in the case of Schnitzler's sex sophistication, say in such a typical play as "Intermezzo," we find the heartbreak of innocent children absurdly dressed as adults bringing down the curtain, while in the case of Anzengruber's idyllic sex, in such a typical play as "The Pastor of Kirchfeld," we find the curtain falling on the heartbreak of adults tempered by a spirit of challenge. I have not, surely, artfully picked out plays that conveniently prove my theory. Fifty, a hundred, others are ready to hand. Compare, for instance, the sophisticated sex plays of de Caillavet and de Flers with the relatively unsophisticated sex plays of such modern Spanish dramatists as Guimera. Compare the sophisticated sex plays of the Hungarian Vajda—"The Little Angel," "Grounds For Divorce" and "Fata Morgana"—with the unsophisticated sex plays of the Hungarian Pasztor—"Innocence," "The Song Eternal," etc. Compare Alfred Capus in this respect with his fellow-countryman Bataille, or Lennox Robinson with his fellow-countryman Synge. Or even the M. Avery Hopwood with the M. Samuel Shipman.

Dramatic indignation, like a show of moral indignation, is often made to serve as a cloak for a species of sex theme that would lodge a tranquil comedy writer in the calaboose. The sophisticated playwright is simply one who, appreciating that indignation is the handmaiden of limited experience, casts his lines in still waters, waters that ever run deeper than the more turbulent streams. He knows out of his contact with the world and its people that sentiment is not less sentiment because it smiles and that there is often more wisdom in laughter than in grunts. The man who laughs over immorality is at heart usually a moral and a sentimental fellow. The man who takes sex as a grim business is pretty generally a man with a foul corner in his mind.

A second adjective in the critical vocabulary that has come to be misused is *literary*. The adjective *sophisticated*, as has been observed, has come to be attached to any play whose author does not believe that adultery is inevitably confined to ketchup and who, in addition, addresses his play to the adult intelligence and emotion rather than to the species of intelligence and emotion that finds its highest pleasure and satisfaction in plays wherein virtue is its own reward, and no questions asked. In the same general way, the adjective *literary* is employed to denominate any otherwise sufficiently dramatic play in which the author has been indiscreet enough to incorporate a few disturbing allusions to novelists and painters, and a set of characters who, in the matter of dialogue, take it for granted that the English language will be intelligible both to themselves and to the audience without borrowing phrases and ejaculations from the contemporaneous bordello, ten-cent lunch room and college campus. The literary play, precisely speaking, is some such also profoundly dramatic play as O'Neill's "The

Great God Brown" or Franz Werfel's "Goat Song."
In these, the so-called literary note is not a surface note, as it is in the case of the plays customarily dubbed literary, but is an integral part of
the dramatic text. In the O'Neill and Werfel
plays, we have literature in terms of drama; in
the other exhibits we have drama in terms of mere
superficial literary trickery. The authors of the
latter plays usually tell their stories as any un-
literary playmaker would tell them, and then go
about hiding the fact by prinking them up with
literary quotations and allusions and with references to traditions and events unfamiliar to customers of crook plays and corn-belt novels. If
such devices constitute a literary play, then a half
dozen pistol shots constitute a dramatic one.

As for sophistication in regard to sex—which
latter generally takes the dramatic form of an
attempt at seduction—such an attempt as we get it
in, say, a Sardou play seems to me five times more
"sophisticated" than the attempt as we get it in,
say, a Guitry play. The tribe of Sardous abandon
preliminaries almost entirely and cause their characters to go bluntly about the deplorable business
like so many Tia Juana saloon-keepers. The
Guitrys, on the other hand, cause their characters
to proceed after the manner of a couple sitting
down to a piano duet. The one method is born

of sophistication all compact; the other, of experienced innocence.

§ 23

With "Still Waters," Mr. Augustus Thomas has now at length been officially lowered into the grave in which, apparently unbeknownst to the majority of writers on the American theatre, he has been peacefully resting for the last twenty-five years. In other words, it has taken American dramatic criticism just one-quarter of a century to arrive at the conclusion that Mr. Thomas, the so-called dean of our dramatists, is what he always has been: a playwright utterly without any authentic talent save the most obvious melodramatic kind. The phenomenon of the gentleman's acceptance as a dramatist of quality is one of the most fetching instances of comic relief in the opera bouffe of American criticism. That he possessed any sound dramatic gifts was, of course, palpably absurd from the day he first entered the American theatre. Yet his acceptance as the first dramatic genius of his country was so widespread that a glance at the reasons therefor may not be unprofitable.

Thomas appeared on the local dramatic scene when the serious stages of the country were given over chiefly to the works of foreign playwrights,

218

most of whom were being vehemently denounced
by the William Winters of the time as lascivious
swine, and worse. Critics and public alike were
ready to acclaim any American, however humble,
who would make a show of dealing with themes
closer to the native pulse. Herne, who preceded
Thomas, showed clearly which way the wind was
blowing. A fifth-rate playwright, he was yet
anointed as an appointee of God. Bronson Howard, who preceded Herne, also a fifth-rater, was
treated as hospitably as if he were a genius of
the first carat. But these men did not entirely
satisfy the critical craving for a true Mahomet.
Howard, after all, even some of the critics realized, was an imitation Englishman whose claims
to being regarded as an American smelling richly
of the soil lay in dressing up the characters in a
Sardou melodrama in blue and gray uniforms and
shifting the scene to the Shenandoah Valley, and
in taking a conventional European farce-comedy
and arbitrarily pasting upon it the title, "Saratoga." And Herne, while indubitably American
so far as calico dresses, down East drawl and can-
vas painted to look like a neighboring lighthouse
went, lacked finish: he was an even greater rhetor-
ical yokel than his themes. What was wanted,
what was prayed for, was an American playwright
who would combine the pseudo-raciness of a Herne

with the English air of a Howard. And in answer to these prayers the Lord sent Mr. Thomas.

Mr. Thomas, accordingly, was swallowed at one gulp, and without a chaser. He was swallowed with such alacrity, indeed, that the critics and public didn't even stop to study the label on the bottle. Thus, he was promptly accepted as a dramatist American to the core on the simple ground that he took a typical German military melodrama of the period, the scene of which was laid in a well-sprinkled German garrison town, covered the coats and leggings of the characters with powdered borax and called the result "Arizona," and as a dramatist thoroughly native yet with the envied English finish on the equally simple ground that he took a typical French theme, deleted the boudoir, caused the characters to speak their lines very slowly and put a note in the program assuring the audience that it was all taking place in Mizzouri or Alabama. But the dam had broken, and the deluge was on: Thomas was the saviour of the American drama. Even then, true enough, there were a few persons who could not quite get the connection between a great dramatic genius and a man who wrote plays in which the solution of profound human torment hung upon the discovery that the bullet that killed the villain was of a different calibre from the hero's

220

revolver and in which a ham actor in a broad
black felt hat, with a false white goatee pasted on
his chin and a manner of speech that brought
every *you* to be followed by an *all* was offered as
the leading chivalrous representative of a great
Southern state and a noble character solely because he was touched by the beauty of the moon.
But the majority of the great American people
and of their cultural guides, the critics, thought
otherwise, and Mr. Thomas settled himself a bit
farther back on his throne.

Mr. Thomas, of course, as any other man in his
place, was not long in persuading himself to accept himself at the value the critics had placed
upon him. And it was not long, accordingly, before he got what our colored brethren call the
profounds. That he was a genius, he did not for
a minute doubt; but that genius should content itself with these relatively modest dramatic offerings was unthinkable. Thus cogitating, our friend
promptly transmuted himself into a great meta-
physician, one who should spread messages to his
people and, out of his deep wisdom, cure them of
their psychic and other ills. This meditation,
with its triumphant consequences in the form of
dramatic art, our friend had preceded with divers
bijoux, merely by way of proving his versatility
in the field of which he was master. These were

—simply as so many *pourboires,* one must understand—little things in which little girls in white nighties crept down into the parlor and held long and sweetly moving conversations with burglars, in which prize-fighters were shown to have hearts of gold beneath their uncouth exteriors, in which Earls of Pawtucket were, for all their spats and monocles, demonstrated to be not such a bad sort, and in which Gallic peccadilloes were disinfected under such titles as "A Proper Impropriety." But, we must remember, these were a master's casual diversions—baubles, mere nothings—tossed off as a bloodhound shakes off the rain water before plunging into the deep Ohio to grab Eliza by the skirt-tail. All this while, the heavy thinking was going on. All this while there were being pondered the really great dramas that were to establish their creator's eminence beyond cavil.

There came then presently from the master-dramatist a succession of great works which, as he had well known they would, lifted him to a dizzy and dismaying altitude in the critical estimation. There was "The Witching Hour," that art work *par excellence* in which a decision of the Supreme Court of the United States was influenced and directed by the ghost of a woman thirty years dead. There was "Mrs. Leffingwell's Boots," that profound document in neo-pathology in which

222

osteopathy cured a case that had baffled the world's great scientific and medical minds. There was "The Harvest Moon," that rich document in psychochromatology in which the course of a woman's life was completely altered for the better by the simple and somehow peculiarly not hitherto thought of device of changing the color of the portières in her room. There was "As A Man Thinks," that scholarly treatise on contemporary economics in which it was proclaimed that if it were not for men's pure love for women all the factories would shut down and no trains would run on schedule. There was "Mere Man," that enduring politico-sociological masterpiece in which it was proved conclusively that men in trying situations always think the way their women will them to think. And there was "The Model," that presented to the world the astounding doctrine that if a girl goes out and has an affair with a man her parents, when they learn of it, will be very sore. Small wonder, then, that the new generation of critics fell in with the order that had passed and added further laurel leaves to Mr. Thomas' already ample crown.

At about this time in our hero's career, however, a great calamity befell American dramatic criticism. A number of the dignified old gentlemen, gifted in the technic of concealing ignorance in polysyllables, who held important critical posts, began one by one to disappear from the scene. Death and intelligent managing editors, those two grim reapers, began to take their toll. And in the places of the departed one presently found young men who could not convince themselves that mere Americanism and dramatic merit were inseparable, that patriotism was an essential part of criticism and that a man with impressive gray hair, a sizeable belly and a bass voice was necessarily a brother to genius. These upstarts were not impressed by honorary degrees confered by road colleges upon men who wrote plays in which the villain was unable to pull the trigger of a revolver merely because the hero looked him in the eye and told him he couldn't, by the otherwise estimable Dr. Brander Matthews' fraternal endorsement of a dramatist simply because the latter belonged to the same club that he did, or by a playwright who sported at his lapel the same purple and yellow ribbon worn by such prodigies in other fields as Robert W. Chambers, Hermann Hagedorn and "Chimmie Fadden" Townsend. And these young impudentos were not long in getting their deplorable convictions into print. If this dean of American dramatists is the fellow we have been told he is, said they, let us investigate him with proper seriousness and lay the bouquets of our findings at his feet. With proper seriousness, they then duly investigated him and, out of that proper seriousness, came the bouquets —of tomatoes *surprises*. For not only did they find that the dean's works of the past had utterly nothing in them, but, in addition, that the works he was then confecting were even emptier than those that had gone before. There was, for example, the play called "As A Man Thinks" which, they observed, was little more than a cheap sentimentalization of the Jews by way of cajoling them out of their easily flattered money at the box-office window. There was, for example, the play called "Indian Summer," in which the same old "Witching Hour" villain was restrained from pulling the trigger of a pistol by the same old "Witching Hour" hero's medicine-show hypnotism act and in which the action revolved around an illegitimate child out of the French mush of the early '70's. There was the play called "The Battle Cry," with its dime-novel Kentucky feud plot and its reliance upon moving pictures to work up a climax. There was the play called "Rio Grande," a twenty-thirty military meller that plainly strove to summon the mildewed corpse of "Arizona" out of its grave. There were "The Copperhead," an old-time "spy" melodrama that dragged in Abe Lincoln by way of getting the boob applause; "Palmy Days," a *mousse* of ham sentimentality with a dog conspicuously inserted into it by way of hokum; and "Nemesis," the big scene of which lay in the same significant gradual dimming of the lights in the death-house at Sing Sing that the fathers of these young men had seen years before in a Hal Reid provincial melodrama. And the sound of the slapstick began to be heard in the land. And a panic seized the Thomas rear.

"Still Waters," as I have noted, is the symbol of that panic. For when a man is panic-stricken, he betrays himself. And "Still Waters" is Mr. Thomas' automatic Judas. It shows up completely and for all time, as with a revolving mirror, the emptiness of his pretensions since the day he first set foot upon the American stage. It shows up brilliantly his sophomoric thought, his sophomoric propaganda indignation, his sophomoric dramatic talent. It crystallizes in a single manuscript the history of his pathetic futility in his chosen field. It is, in a flash, an autobiography of the Thomas dramaturgy from 1880 to the present day.

WHAT'S WRONG WITH THE THEATRE

Treatises on what's wrong with the theatre appear with the regularity of dramatic critics' need for an extra hundred dollars. Aside from the obvious fact that one of the chief things wrong with the theatre is three-quarters of its dramatic critics, I have been unable to dredge up from these articles anything but stenciled, useless and utterly asinine generalities. We are told, for example, that the theatre is in a bad way because the moving pictures and the radio have robbed it of a very considerable share of its former audiences. Just how the merciful removal from the theatre of such fathomless mushheads as venerate celluloid mugging and dephlogisticated jazz above one of the finest of the seven arts may be regarded as a damage to the theatre is surely a problem for a professor of the higher logic. We are told, again, that the theatre has been commercialized to such a degree that it has lost caste, and is today fit only for susceptible fat women and men more or less immunized to its flapdoodle by ethyl alcohol. Nothing could be farther from the truth. The

New York theatre of today, taking it by and large, is less commercialized than it has been for thirty years. Of the fifty-eight legitimate theatres in New York at the present time, not more than a dozen, estimating them one year with another, may be said to be consecrated wholly and absolutely to commercial excreta. Of the ten legitimate theatres in New York thirty years ago, five were for the most part merely markets for such excreta. The deduced ratio is thus approximately forty-six to five.

We are told, further, that, commercialized stages or no commercialized stages, so much rubbish has been produced in the last half-dozen years that intelligent audiences have been weaned from the theatre and no longer patronize it. Yet just as much rubbish, proportionately, was produced thirty years ago, as a glance at the records will clearly demonstrate, and just as many intelligent persons were alienated then as now. Again, we are told that three-quarters of our playwrights currently write with an eye to the moving picture possibilities of their plays and that, as a result, their wares are debased. Yet three-quarters of our playwrights of thirty years ago, before the moving pictures appeared on the scene, were similarly merely cheap salesmen out for the box-office money, and their plays were just as bad as those which the present-day playwright confects with the screen in the back of his mind. Still again, we are told that the over-supply of theatres and the under-supply of good plays have brought the theatre to a low artistic level. Yet no one would think of employing any such idiotic argument against American literature, although there are presently an over-supply of publishers as great as the over-supply of theatres and an equal under-supply of good books. One can no more fairly estimate the theatre by listing its every ten bad plays against its solitary good one than one can estimate the native literature by listing its every hundred bad novels against its solitary respectable one. Continuing, we are told that, aside from the so-called small theatre groups like the Guild, Greenwich Village Theatre, Stagers, et cetera, our producers are in the main concerned very little with dramatic merit and devote themselves largely to such plays as will appeal to the biggest audiences. Yet those who argue in this direction overlook the fact that, a comparatively short time ago, we didn't have even the small theatre groups that we have today and hence were then not half so well off as we are at present.

I set down a few sample laments; they suggest the many others that are too familiar to call for rehearsal. And, as I have observed, almost all

of them are quickly found to be true only superficially; at bottom, they are empty. The simple
truth is that what is wrong with the theatre today is what has been wrong with the theatre
always, and what, doubtless, will continue to
be wrong with it until Gabriel plays his cornet
solo. What is wrong with the theatre lies almost wholly in the heads of its critics. The
theatre is all right; the difficulty is that its critics
expect altogether too much of it. Here is a toy,
the greatest toy the world has ever known, as a toy
begun and as a toy continued, that they would
have other than it actually is in its bottommost
core. Theirs is a beautiful dream and a beautiful
hope, but so were the dream and hope, the impossible dream and hope, of the Egyptians that
Diocletian burned. The alchemy that might trans-
mute into gold that half of the theatre which is
tinsel is not within the gift of mortal man, and
perhaps providentially. For a toy has need of
its share of tinsel; a jumping-jack of gold would
be an absurd paradox. The theatre, being a toy,
is not for philosophers as philosophers, but only
for men sufficiently wise to be periodically foolish.
It is something for grown men to play with when
the mood of seriousness is not upon them, and when
they would listen to music with their eyes and,
blindfolded, look at life through their ears. Why

seek to change that which cannot and which should not be changed? The theatre lives atop the monument of its very faults.

Something, as has been noted, is always wrong with the theatre. If it isn't said to be the Syndicate that, in its day, was supposed to be throttling the life out of it, it is said to be the star system that, in its day, was supposed similarly to be throttling the life out of it. Each decade supplies its reason for what is wrong with the theatre, and still the theatre, as an institution, prospers as it has never prospered before. All the convincing reasons assigned for the failure of marriage haven't killed marriage. All the convincing reasons assigned for the ending of war have never stopped war. All the convincing reasons assigned for the wrongness of the theatre will never keep the theatre from going on its bland and engaging way. Duly appreciating which, let us take a look at a few things that are actually wrong with the American theatre at the present moment, and then promptly forget them. Some of these things are apparently trivial, and some of them are not new, but they are in combination doing more to disgust persons with the theatre than half of the more important reasons indignantly set forth by the composers of the treatises to which I have refered.

In the first place, there is the matter of the con-

duct of the box-office and the selling of tickets. A
man goes to the box-office and asks for a seat not
farther than six rows removed from the stage.
Assuming that any good seats are left in the box-
office, which is of course highly unlikely, he will
be given one in row F, which a covert digital count
will reassure him is, surely enough, in the sixth
row. When he gets into the theatre subsequently,
he will find time and again that the first four or
five rows have double letters and that row F is
not the sixth row, but the tenth or eleventh. Or he
will go to a ticket agency, as I have gone on occasion, will buy a seat with the assurance that
it is "just one off the aisle" and, taking the clerk's
word for it and putting the ticket into his pocket,
will subsequently find that it is a selling trick of
the agency's to consider seats in pairs and group
each two as a unit, and that his seat is accordingly
not the second seat off the aisle, but the fifth.
Again, he will buy a seat at the box-office, will
complain that it is too far back, and will be told
that there are only twelve rows in the theatre and
that his seat is thus in, say, what would be the
seventh or eighth row at any other theatre. And
he will subsequently find that the theatre has
twenty rows and that he is lucky if he can catch
even an occasional glimpse of the stage.

For all the loud talk of the district attorney's

office relative to the prosecution of ticket agencies that charge more than a fifty-cent premium on tickets, it is still impossible to get the prefered positions in a theatre from these agencies unless one pays anywhere from one to five dollars more than the price stamped on the ticket. One can get tickets with the fifty-cent advance for some theatres, but not for a single theatre whose attraction is in demand. The agencies, many of them, have a list of charge patrons who they know will not betray them, and for these they hold out the good seats at a fancy swindle. Such agencies as do not have charge lists turn over their best seats for the big attractions to "blinds" and these dispose of them at exorbitantly advanced prices. If the "blinds" are apprehended, they have nothing to lose, as they are not licensed brokers and hence obviously cannot have their licenses taken away from them. They may be fined twenty-five or fifty dollars, which the agency, remaining under cover, pays for them and then, with a well-satisfied chuckle, promptly goes about hiring new "blinds" to take their places.

After one gets into a theatre, what happens? One goes with the peace of God in one's heart and perhaps even a good cocktail in one's middle, prepared to enjoy an evening in comfort. One takes one's program and turns to the cast of characters.

But it isn't there. One looks again and still cannot find it. One wonders. One doesn't recall that many persons tear out this part of a playbill for souvenir or future reference and that, after the show is over, the ushers economically pick up the old programs, smooth them out and pass them out again the next night. And then, just as one has contrived to regain one's composure by the exercise of five or six soul-satisfying cuss words, a draught, laden with influenza, pneumonia or, if one is lucky, a mere terrible cold in the head, hits one directly in the back of the neck. The theatre has been improved one thousand per cent in the last twenty years; the architects have developed their art wonderfully; the genius of producers the world over has brought into being a stage rapidly nearing perfection; acoustics are better than they have ever been before; chair designers have managed the ultimate in the physical comfort of the human rachis; interior decorators have beautified the scene. But, though millions upon millions of dollars have been spent and though the theatre of today is to the theatre of yesterday what Buckingham Palace is to a Mills Hotel, no genius apparently has yet been found who can put weatherstrips on the doors in such wise that stiff necks and chilblains are not the price of the modern

Shakespeare or George Cohan. Again, with the growing custom of women's smoking in the lobby between the acts, the doors of a theatre are thrown wide open at such times on the coldest nights of Winter, with the result that any man who doesn't wish to go out and listen to the conversation of idiots or any woman sufficiently well-mannered to stay in her seat is half-frozen by the time the curtain goes up again.

We come thus to the audience or, more particularly, the first-night audience. The respectable New York first-night audience went down on the *Lusitania* with Charles Frohman. When Frohman passed from the theatrical scene, the decent first-night audience passed with him. Here and there, a trace of it still remains, but for the most part it has gone, where, no one seems to know. There is a trace of its old brilliance at a Morris Gest opening, a Dillingham opening, a Ziegfeld opening and, sometimes, at a Winthrop Ames or Arthur Hopkins opening, but, in major measure, the seats that once were filled by well-dressed, clean-looking, cultured men and women are now occupied by moving-picture magnates and their agents, snooping for possible material for their screens, by sandwich-restaurant operators luxuriating in unaccustomed dinner jackets and by modistes who run houses of call as a side-line and are on the look-out for new material behind the footlights.

I have hinted at the recent heavy encroachment upon the theatre by the motion picture morons. I shall not go further into the situation at this point. But one thing is certain. Although in the end these pimps of drama may not succeed in doing the evil to the theatre that they have their hearts set upon, the widespread knowledge that they have got their hands on the American stage will operate to keep thousands of persons out of the theatre for some time to come. Already, indeed, we have plenty of signs to show which way the wind is turning. Among my friends, for example, I number eight who, for the last twelve years, have had regular orders with their ticket-agents for seats at fourteen specific New York playhouses. Since the news of the movie-backed theatrical enterprises has been published, all have canceled their orders for all but four of the theatres, preferring not to trust the producers in question as heretofore but to wait and learn precisely what kind of stuff they were going to offer. Surely, this can be no isolated case. On every hand one hears the doubters. The worst thing that has happened to the American theatre in our time happened to it the day the newspapers printed the intelligence that the Famous Players company had taken over the Charles Frohman enterprises, whether the Famous Players company betters or ruins those enterprises or not, and the day, following that, when the newspapers printed the information that the Fox company was about to back a number of producers hitherto independent. As I say, it may not all matter much in the long run,—that, we shall learn in due time,—but for the next few years the theatre as an institution will suffer sorely. A few of the movie-backed producers may get rich, but for every two dollars they put into their pockets the theatre will eventually be one theatregoer poorer.

As for the road, as it is called, the present deplorable state in which the provincial theatre finds itself is too well known to warrant extended comment. The road, practically speaking, has almost ceased to exist and the American theatre has come to signify merely the New York theatre. What has brought this state of affairs about? The reasons customarily assigned do not especially convince me. We are told that the quality of plays sent out by the managers is so low that road audiences have gradually become sickened and have, in despair, given up going to the theatre save when something first-class is vouchsafed them. Yet in the last three years, out of the twenty-four respectable plays produced in New York, sixteen have been sent on the road, production and cast intact, and fourteen of these have been rank commercial failures. We are told, again, that the road is tired of being fooled with inferior companies and declines longer to be swindled. But the records show that even when the New York companies are shown and provincial theatregoers are duly convinced of the fact, the patronage is not sufficient to keep the presentation alive. Still further, we are told that, in the instance of the smaller and better musical comedies, the orchestras engaged at the various road theatres are not up to standard and so aggravate the sensitive provincial musical ear. Yet if musical comedy audiences, whether in New York or anywhere else, know enough about music to tell a really good orchestra from one that is only so-so, I should like to have one such audience identified to me. I doubt, as I say, that any of these reasons or any of the others like them which find their way into the controversial prints are at the bottom of the collapse of the provincial theatre. That theatre, I believe, is where it is today for reasons much more obvious and very much simpler. The trouble with the road theatres lies not so much in what goes on on their stages as in the theatres themselves. With just six lonely and estimable exceptions that I can think of, there isn't a so-called first-class theatre on the road that isn't so physically dirty that to sit in it for two hours is to come out feeling and looking like the bottom of a Neapolitan spittoon. Proscenium curtains that haven't been dusted since McKinley's time, chairs with the plush so worn that one's nether-anatomy rests upon the substratum of prickly excelsior and the backs of which are thick with mementoes of hair salve and perspiration, carpets so filthy that they eat through shoe-leather, a general empyreuma akin to that of a cow-stable—such is the average house of illusion that one encounters up and down the countryside. It is no secret, indeed, that the biggest purchasers of rat-traps and rat-poison have come to be these provincial theatres. Ten years, fifteen years, twenty and thirty years, they go along without improvements of any kind, rotting out of neglect. With washrooms that no white man would dare to venture into, with drinking water weeks old in dirt-covered bottles, with lobbies dimly lighted to cut down electrical bills, with slovenly female ushers hesitating on their way to seat locations to shift their wads of chewing-gum and to hitch up their garters, with a cheap and wheezy mechanical music-machine in the pit once occupied by an orchestra, with programs printed on a single strip of cheap paper and the cheap ink of which comes off on one's fingers, with the heat-

239

ing apparatus turned on only a few minutes before eight o'clock and that thus drowns out the play with its banging until after nine, and with the illumination in front of the house economically turned off before the audience is entirely in, these theatres yet speculate why it is that people prefer to go across the way to the new, brightly lighted, clean and perfectly conducted moving picture theatres. A theatre must be a theatre even before its curtain goes up on drama. It must have glamor and illusion and wonder. These road theatres are less theatres than pig-wallows. On that day when the managers of the provincial theatres hire competent scrubwomen, put an extra dozen incandescent bulbs in their lobbies and supply their women ushers with a reliable deodorant, on that day and not until that day will the road again show signs of prosperity. Meanwhile, the plays of Eugene O'Neill and men like him will fail on the road quite as promptly as the plays of the meanest hacks. It is every bit as unpleasant and souring to come away from "Hamlet" with a large grease-spot on the seat of your pants as it is to come away from "Mutt and Jeff."

THE AMERICAN TASTE

Although it is unquestionably true that American taste on its higher levels has shown a considerable advance in the last twenty or thirty years, it is equally true that that taste on its second, third and fourth levels has in the same period of time shown an amazing decline. I doubt, in point of fact, if the taste of the average American has ever been at such low ebb as it is today. What psychic phenomenon has brought this state of affairs about, I have—doubtless contrary to your anticipation—not the faintest idea. But that it exists, even a most cursory survey of the present scene makes evident, and that the immediate future contains rosier symptoms, only one long skilled in the legerdemain of optimism can persuade himself.

The American landscape presents currently the spectacle of a slaughter-house of taste unequaled, in degree and magnitude, anywhere else in the civilized world. The view is of an unbroken succession of abattoirs, each bursting with the profits of its depravity. The newsstands throughout the land are stacked daily, as never before, with hundreds of periodicals beside which the cheapest and most vulgar magazines of twenty years ago were symposia of transcendent æsthetics. Scores of gaudy brochures which profess to recount the true bedroom and hayloft experiences of Swedish servant girls, stenographers, chorus girls and Y. W. C. A. workers; dozens upon dozens of small magazines with such names as "Hot Puppy," "Oh Baby!", "Peppy Pips" and the like, which publish jokes and stories that deal with *crim. con.* and the delights of the key-hole; manifold whiz-bangs which, under the cloak of moral indignation, retail lascivious scandals; countless so-called art portfolios made up of photographs of stripped chorus girls with apparently accidental smudges of printers' ink carefully registered in such spots as to cause stampedes of prurientos to the newsstands from miles 'round; imitations of risqué French publications with rear views of fat women and front views of thin ones; innumerable so-called snappy magazines whose covers announce such titles as "Why Myrtle Did It," "After Eight Cocktails" and "Roll Over on Your Side, Dearie"; scores of others with covers showing terrified blondes in the coils of boa constrictors, with seven-foot cowboys charging to the rescue; dozens of still others with such titular fillips as "Love Se-

crets," "Marriage Secrets" and "Secret Secrets"
—of such is the flood of literary and graphic
sewage that presently waters the culture of the
country. Twenty years ago, the magazines that
entertained the average American were, at their
worst, those which muckraked the Standard Oil
Company, exposed the frenzied finance of Wall
Street and published pictures of Lulu Glaser.
Today, the magazines that entertain the average
American are those in which a choir soprano tells
what the sexton tried to do to her after buying
her two frosted vanillas, in which retired ladies
of joy and politicians give away their dead friends
and protectors of other days, and in which the
"art section" is made up of nude photographs of
nondescript, but shapely, little girls who have left
the hay and feed towns of the Middle West, en-
trained for Hollywood in quest of fame and millions, and ended up as five dollar a day (and ten
dollar a night) mermaids, nymphs and sirens in
the aquatic movie master-gems.

The moving pictures themselves have made tre-
mendously successful strides forward in the last
few years in corrupting further the nation's taste
and intelligence. It is now some six years since
I observed, in a paper called "The Hooligan at
the Gate," that it would not be long before the
cinema bilge would so soak into every nook and

243

corner of the land that the æsthetic content of the
mind of the community, then estimated at about
one-half of one per cent, would soon be reduced to
.000000$\frac{1}{10}$ per cent. What was predicted has happened. The torrent of movie scum has swept all
vestiges of taste, or what conceivably might some
day have developed into taste, from the countryside. It has, with the bursting of its garbage-dam,
carried with it what was left of the dramatic theatre
in all save three American cities, until today what
is known in theatrical parlance as "the road" is, as
I observed in the preceding chapter, practically
non-existent. With the exception of these few
remaining cities in which respectable drama can
still get a precarious hearing and fitfully make
enough, perhaps, to pay its way, there isn't a
town in the Republic that has enough taste and
intelligence left in it to allow a first-rate play to
last out the week. A dirty bedroom farce, an
all-star fake, a leg show, a dramatic gimcrack
or a piece of trumpery featuring a conspicuous
trouper—these are here and there able to draw
audiences outside of New York, Chicago and one
or two other centres, but anything of moderate
merit, save perhaps occasionally a Walter Hamp-
den Shakespearian troupe, doesn't stand any more
chance than a Ku Kluxer in Liberia. The movies,
nine hundred and ninety-nine out of every one

thousand of which are the veriest dramatic ditch-water, have slowly drowned the dramatic taste of the nation until today all that is left of it is a gurgle and a few bubbles. Indeed, so thoroughly have the movies done their job that the American taste is no longer able to appreciate even a respect-able moving picture. "The Last Laugh," a worthy piece of work so far as moving pictures go, thus could hardly make enough money outside of New York to pay for Will Hays' cigars.

Supporting the cheap magazines and moving pictures in their campaign to moronize the coun-try, we have now the radio. The roofs of houses from the Atlantic to the Pacific presently take on the aspect of so many sailless schooners. And nightly the front parlors of the boobletariat re-sound to the strains of alley jazz pounded out by bad hotel orchestras, to lectures on Christian Science by ex-veterinary surgeons, to songs about red hot mamas and Beale Street megrims by hard-up vaudeville performers, and to the names of the notables who have just come into Reuben's delicatessen restaurant. Where, a few years ago, a family living in the hinterland occasionally after dinner read a book or at least looked through an album of "Famous Masterpieces of Painting," it presently glues receivers to its ears and is thrown into wild æsthetic transports by some Harlem coon's *recitativo* on his *Heimweh* for Alabamy or some two-a-day master artist's interpretation of Bach on a ukulele. There are two radio broadcasting stations, one in New York and one in Philadelphia, that have made an effort periodically to give their customers something better in the way of music than that which, for its finest effect, must be played on kitchen utensils and cowbells and something better in the way of educational talks than lectures on hygiene by press-agents for new mouth-washes, but I understand that they have found the going rough and, in self-preservation, have been forced to fall back more and more on the gibberish and caterwauling that the ether connoisseurs admire.

As first aid to these several agents in the brilliant debasing of the American public, there has entered lately the tabloid newspaper. A tabloid newspaper, you need not be told, is a newspaper reduced in size, sense, taste and decency. The majority of these newly born journals are simply so many cheaply illustrated *Broadway Brevities* given over to the two C's with which the English are wont to describe a certain yellow 'un published by the eminent Lord Riddell. They are, the most of them, scandal sheets pure and simple masquerading as newspapers behind an occasional editorial on the League of Nations and an oc-

246

casional photograph of General Pershing dedicating a new lodge of Moose or of Cal Coolidge shaking hands with Al Jolson. Their pages are given over to stories of rape in the Baptist belt, sensational divorce cases, news of drug peddlers, advice to stenographers on sex and love, dream charts, horoscopes, numerology tables showing how a man may become a Rockefeller by changing his name from Moritz to Guido and how a woman may become a Ninon de l'Enclos by reducing the number of letters in her Christian name from six to three and thus becoming Mae instead of Lizzie, and other such journalistic *entremets*, the whole promiscuously illustrated with badly reproduced cuts of women escaping from fires in négligé, prize-fighters in jock-straps and congressmen and chorus girls sailing for Europe. These journals, spreading rapidly from city to city, are cutting more and more deeply into the circulation of the old, reputable papers as the lowered public taste licks its chops over them. And they are serving admirably to drag that taste lower and lower still to the bottom of the dump.

Among the many reasons assigned for the remarkable popular success of these tabloid newspapers, I fail to detect one, incidentally, that doubtless snuggles closer to the core than all the others. To say that the tabloids have succeeded because the public likes pictures, or prefers its news boiled down to a couple of sticks, or itches for sensationalism, or has found the large-size, standard journals too unwieldly, or prefers 12-point type to 8-point, is either to aim at the bull's-eye with generalities, mostly false, or to chase one's tail arguing that a thing is true because it apparently isn't untrue. If the public likes pictures above all things, why were *Burr McIntosh's Monthly*, the original *Collier's Weekly* and *Leslie's Weekly*, pioneers and leaders among latter-day picture publications, such dismal failures? If the public doesn't like large and unwieldly publications, why are the New York *Times* and the *Saturday Evening Post* such tremendous successes? If the public likes large and not small type, why does this same *Saturday Evening Post* enjoy such unparalleled prosperity? If it is merely sensationalism that the public relishes, why are not Hearst papers like the New York *American*, more successful than they are and why was Enright's New York *Bulletin* driven to the ash-heap in such quick order?

The success of the tabloids may rest in part upon these principles, but only in part. The tabloids have succeeded for another and plainer reason. The public, or at least that great proportion of the public that has taken up these illustrated *demi-blatts,* is the same public that had hitherto rested its pursuit of intelligence and culture entirely upon the old-time yellow press. The latter, as is known, enjoyed an unprecedented reign of popularity for many years and then suddenly showed signs of a violent seizure of cholera morbus and began slipping rapidly down the coal-chute. What brought this decline about was its peculiar public's cumulative loss of faith in its honesty, for even a public like that which devoured the yellows is not entirely without goat-sense. This public, duped for years with fraud and fake, with murders, seductions, kidnappings, robberies, Black Hand bands, Jack-the-Rippers, mysterious wild men and ghosts that never took place or never existed, finally caught on to the leg-pulling that was going on and refused any longer to buy tickets for the show. And at that moment the small illustrated newspaper, which is an even bigger fake than the old yellow newspaper, was born.

And why? Because pictures don't lie. Or at least the boob doesn't think they lie. He no longer believes anything he *reads* in the newspapers, but he believes everything he *sees*. A photograph showing him an Indiana detective shooting "Dutch" Anderson (carefully posed up an alley by a couple of reporters) seems to him a much

more accurate piece of intelligence about the day's
news than an article which is similarly very largely
the product of a reporter's imagination. An old
photograph of Carrie Nation that is made to pass
for one of Ma Ferguson, a photograph of the
Battle of Manila Bay with the caption "The
United States Navy Goes After the Rum Fleet,"
a picture of the last Armistice Day parade headed
"The Funeral of Frank A. Munsey," or the re-
production of a movie still of "East Lynne" with
the inscription "Mrs. Stillman Denies She Will
Re-Wed Husband" is entirely convincing to the
boob who no longer trusts the news of the day set
forth in mere printer's type. And thus it is that
such papers as Hearst's *American* decline in circulation while such as Hearst's *Mirror* go shooting up.

That the public taste, while now lower than it
has ever been, is thus steadily getting lower and
lower, there can be small doubt. The theatre, true
enough, is but one of many microscopes through
which to view the bacilli, but it, too, may serve its
purpose in throwing its gleam of illumination
upon the scene. In such a case, of course, it is
always the answer of the bravo-dispensers to point
ironically to the estimable MM. Collier, Cibber
and other such indignant fellows and apologists
of centuries bygone and mockingly to observe that

the theatre has consistently been going to the dogs ever since ushers began showing Greeks to the wrong seats back in the Fifth Century B. C. But the fact remains that while the theatre of New York City is better today than it ever was, the theatre of the rest of America has never, so far as popular taste goes, been in worse shape. The ledgers in the Erlanger and Shubert offices offer ample testimony to the sad fact that never before has a decent piece of dramatic writing experienced such tough sledding out of New York as it experiences today. In the season that began on September 1, 1925, and ended on June 1, 1926, for example, just one admittedly good play managed to survive a comparatively brief road tour. All the others, without exception, failed to draw sufficient audiences to keep them going and had to be recalled and thrown into the storehouse. The theatrical taste of America at the present time is for "Abie's Irish Rose," which is the worst of the popular plays that have prospered most greatly in the American theatre: which is twice as bad as "Way Down East," three times as bad as "Uncle Tom's Cabin," five times as bad as "Ben Hur" and ten times as bad as "Charley's Aunt."

When the average American goes into a theatre today, his taste is not for respectable drama, but for trash. That trash may take the form of a moving picture, a vaudeville show or anything else just so long as it makes no call upon him for imagination, an appreciation of beauty, even a modest amount of intelligence, or an artistic sensitiveness above that of a bologna sausage. The vaudeville business has never been so prosperous as it is at the present moment, and this applies not only to the so-called big-time vaudeville but to the despised small-time as well. Throughout the land countless new vaudeville theatres, as costly and vulgar as the movie palaces, have sprung up on the graves of dramatic theatres and nightly discharge their reinforced batteries of concentrated guano against what is left of native theatrical good-breeding. Where Mansfield once held the provincial stage, a Charleston hoofer now takes a dozen bows. Where Sothern was once brought before the curtain, a trained duck now brings down the thunders of applause. Where fine drama once reigned, there is now but an endless succession of alley-oop Dutchmen, virtuosi of "Pagliacci" on the accordion, jugglers of Japanese parasols, and skits in which the line, "You can come home now; the sheriff's dead," is followed by the speaker's receipt of a kick in the trousers.

The current low ebb of the Republic's taste in general may be ascertained by taking, as an ex-

ample, a single typical city. Since it would perhaps be unfair to take a city whose taste is already suspect to any considerable degree, let us
take one like, say, Boston, which is commonly regarded as the seat of New England culture. The
dramatic taste of this city has been sinking year
by year until today it is on a level with that of a
mill-town. Only hip shows and suggestive bedroom plays longer do any trade; anything first-
rate in the way of drama plays to empty houses.
Things have got to such a pass, indeed, that the
booking offices no longer send any first-rate plays
to Boston. But the cheaper movies flourish there
like fancy women in Norfolk, Va. For the better-
grade moving pictures, the town has no use, but
for the flapdoodle of the screen it supplies enormous audiences. In the way of literary taste, an
investigation made recently by a reporter for the
New York *World* is rich in statistics. This investigation showed that the books in greatest demand at the Boston Public Library at the present
time are those with Wild West and detective plots.
The persons who lead in the demand for these
books are—I quote the person in charge of the
fiction department—"doctors, lawyers, teachers
and business men," that is, not the riff-raff, but
the better class of Bostonians. Among the books
barred by the Boston Public Library are Dreiser's

"Sister Carrie" and "Jennie Gerhardt" and W. S. Maugham's "Of Human Bondage," together with the works of James Joyce, George Moore, Sherwood Anderson and Aldous Huxley. Among those welcomed to the extent of five copies apiece are Elbert Hubbard's "Message to Garcia," Thomas Dixon's "The Clansman," Zane Grey's "Riders of the Purple Sage" and E. M. Hull's "The Sheik." The *World* investigator found further that the non-fiction books most in demand on the request slips were those dealing with, again I quote, "typewriting and will-power." The taste of the patrons of the so-called Open Shelf Room of the library is, the investigator learned, at present overwhelmingly for the "confession" species of books. The tome which enjoyed the largest circulation for the period of six months directly previous to the inquiry was "The Confessions of the Czarina." Outside of the library, Boston's two favorite authors are O. Henry and Harold Bell Wright, with Robert Cortes Holliday and James Oliver Curwood as runners-up. Boston's favorite poet, a careful canvass showed, is Robert Service. Only two copies of Thomas Hardy were sold in Boston in the six months from January 1 to July 1. A canvass of the newsstands disclosed that the favorite weekly was the *Western Story*

Magazine and the favorite monthly, by long odds, *True Stories*.

What is true of Boston is true of most of the rest of America. The stars in the nation's flag have slowly but surely turned into so many Elk's badges. The taste of the nation has become the taste of its shoe dealers and barbers.

BAGATELLES IN C MINOR

§ 1

From time to time, our esteemed theatrical managers go into prolonged conferences with themselves and bring themselves to the conclusion that what is wrong with our revue theatre is its lack of Parisian atmosphere. Having arrived at this conclusion, they promptly set about achieving that atmosphere by dressing up the ticket-taker at the entrance like a French artillery major, inserting a number into the show in which the smaller chorus girls sing a song called "We Wee-wees Always Say Oui-Oui," exhibiting a tableau in which a blonde girl in strip tights lies prostrate at the feet of a fierce chorus man with his face, arms and torso smeared with lamp-black, and putting a sign over the door leading to the men's lavatory reading *"Pour les Messieurs."* This done, they naturally get very sore when, subsequently, the reviewers express certain doubts as to the entire authenticity of the French atmosphere and deliver themselves of uncalled-for remarks about a show entitled "Passetemps Parisiens" whose chief features are a couple of German acrobats, a skit cabbaged from the 1918 edition of the London "Nine o'Clock Revue" and a spectacular number called "The Apotheosis of Baseball."

One of the greatest of present-day American frauds is this so-called French atmosphere which our producers believe they contrive to get into their exhibitions, and an even greater present-day American fraud is the class of reviewers who make fun of what the producers do in the belief that the actual French atmosphere is something much different and vastly more exciting. If the Parisian atmosphere evoked by our producers is approximately as Gallic as a seidel of Pschorrbräu, the Parisian atmosphere evoked by the French producers themselves is equally as Gallic as Broadway and Forty-second Street. What, honestly, is this French atmosphere we hear so much about? After many years' valiant service as one of the heads of the American Expeditionary Force assigned to duty at the Folies Bergère, Olympia, Cigale, Marigny, Moulin Rouge and other such French music halls, I conclude that it amounts to little more than a dozen dirty jokes, some chorus girls in the altogether, a sassy crack at Briand, and a rear promenade in which damsels of joy ogle for trade and in which one may drop a sou into the slot and weigh one's self. The legend of

French atmosphere, of course, is a quite different thing. It conjures up pictures of beautiful women, their skirts around their necks, dancing on the tops of tables, the while gay boulevardiers quaff champagne from their slippers, of handsome lieutenants of Cuirassiers lounging sheikishly on rear divans, puffing lazily at cigarettes filled with opium and making boudoir eyes at the ladies, of a stage so witty that Congreve and Wycherley nightly turn over in their graves, of wenches so aphrodisiacal and devilish that no Paris grandpa has need of Steinach, of tunes as soft and insinuating as so many amorous eels, and of a general air of gaiety and abandon the like of which one can find nowhere else on the earth.

A fetching picture, but one that is, alas, far from the truth! If ever there has been a music hall in Paris, save perhaps the Marigny back in the early 1900's, that has had one-third the hypothetical Parisian atmosphere that Ziegfeld's "Follies" has in New York, I must have been in Munich drinking the waters when it opened its doors. More, such a show as Earl Carroll's "Vanities" is almost everything in the way of French atmosphere that the French revues aren't. True enough, such an opinion will not be coincided in by gentlemen who sum up the phrase "French atmosphere" in the spectacle of a woman *in puris natu-*

ralibus, but it must be agreed to by all such others as have visited the Paris music halls when they weren't too drunk.

I allow myself to believe, further, that the New York audiences that patronize our revues are, in the mass, every bit as carefree and light-hearted, and certainly also as light-headed, as those that go in for the same type of amusement in Paris. These particular New York audiences are wholly different from the New York dramatic audiences. They are made up, in general, of the spenders, drinkers, jazz babies and devotees of metropolitan night-life, and are close in resemblance to the Paris audiences. And what they see on our revue stages is, to repeat, stuff as Frenchy as that on the Paris revue stages is not. The average Paris revue is really three parts American to one part French. It is made up largely of second-rate American vaudeville performers who can't get bookings over here and who find it an easy thing to put over the old hokum on the frogs. And if, on the other hand, our own revues are French only superficially, the American reviewer has small ground for complaint. Our revue jokes and skits are today dirtier than any you'll find in Paris; there is, I hear, just as much opportunity for biological sport among the girls, if one has a mind to such things; and only a measly one-inch strip of gauze stands between our Phrynes and those of the boulevards. It thus seems to me that our producers make a mistake to emphasize the French atmosphere of their revues, and so drive away many sophisticated and experienced theatregoers, when their American revues are actually three or four times better in every respect than the French ones. For one patron they gain in the person of a jackass who prefers an unbathed and bony French hussy in the stark altogether to a clean, shapely American girl in transparent silk veiling, they lose two who have been bored to death in Paris with the Phillips Sisters' old Pantages Circuit clog dances, Harry Pilcer's high kicking and economical reproductions of Ben Ali Haggin's old "Follies" living pictures. Let our producers forget Paris and put on their good shows as straight American shows, and it will not be long before the French kiosks will be plastered with bills advertising Paris revues with the true New York atmosphere.

That the revue form, however, is beginning to lose its erstwhile complete hold on the American public's fancy is a piece of news approximately as fresh and startling as the tidings that Goethe is dead. Yet a brief inquiry into the causes of its malaise may serviceably be undertaken before the hearse backs up. There are, true enough, one or two of the revues that are still attracting crowds but, unless I am greatly mistaken, they are attracting these crowds much as some such other rapidly dying institution as the Ferris Wheel or the bathing beauty contest attracts them. For all the patronage that is being visited upon the few survivors, the pulse of the revue is unmistakably growing feebler month by month and, unless all signs fail—which they sometimes have an embarrassing habit of doing in the case of theatrical criticism—it will not be long before the revue form as we know it today passes into the stage discard along with the Lake Como seduction drama, comedians who work their moustaches up and down with a string, and Hart, Shaffner and Marx Hamlets.

What has spelled the death sentence of the revue is its monotony. Only the recent liberal injections of smut have contrived to keep it alive so long as this. For one exhibit like Charlot's or the "Grand Street Follies" that has brought something new to the species of entertainment in the form of wit, we have had several dozen that have done little more than to repeat themselves year in and year out. And not only have they imitated themselves; they have imitated one another until they are as much alike as so many Italian table d'hôtes. See one and you see them all. There

are the same undraped tableaux allegedly depicting "The Marriage of the Seasons," "The Spirit
of the Gowanus Canal" or something of the sort,
but actually depicting little else than six or seven
hussies with good shapes; there are the same flip-
flop gents and soft-shoe hoofers dug up out of the
minor vaudeville houses; there are the same tire-
some Charleston finales with a stageful of white
flappers unsuccessfully trying to be as skilful as
black wenches; there are the same skits based
upon old and familiar smoking-car wheezes; there
are the same jazz bands brought in from the neighboring supper clubs to give succor to drooping
second acts; there are the same parades of icy
showgirls in diamond nightgowns or borrowed
furs; there are the same numbers about Omar
Khayyam's or some one's else dream in which,
when the tenor gets to the chorus, the lights go
down and through a scrim at the back one glimpses
the same old undressed baggages. This has been
going on now for so long that the public may be
forgiven its symptoms of apathy and its increasing predilection for that form of musical entertainment that approaches the manner of the better-
grade musical comedy. The success of "Blossom
Time," "Wildflower," "Rose-Marie," "The Student
Prince," "Princess Flavia," "The Vagabond King"
and pieces of a kidney plainly shows a turn in the

weather-cock. And thus it would seem that the taste of the public, in the way of theatrical musical entertainment, is reverting to the order of yester-day, quite as the taste of the public indicates a similar reversion in other directions. And thus, further, we find the revue giving ground to musical comedy coincidently with the return to favor of such other favorites of yesterday as the nickel-odeon, unbobbed hair, cowboy fiction, Ibsen and the derby hat.

§ 2

The current indignation of certain musicians on the subject of jazz and their disposition to place it in the musical category somewhere between Schönberg and the American Can Company need not unduly alarm composers who are working seriously in the field. The latter may comfort-ably reflect that even Haydn joined Albrechts-berger in condemning in no uncertain critical lan-guage the license and lawlessness of the destroyer of forms named Beethoven, that Wagner and his disciples considered Brahms something of a jacka-napes, that the operas of Wagner himself were re-jected by opera-house manager after opera-house manager as being utterly impossible and that when "Tannhäuser" was produced in Paris the critics threw so many dead cats onto the stage that it was withdrawn after three performances, that the musicians of the time actually at first refused to dignify the new-fangled instrumental tremolos of Monteverde by consenting to play them, and that some of the professors still swoon and yell for the smelling salts when anyone mentions the name of Richard Strauss.

§ 3

It has been demonstrated by the Theatre Guild and other such organizations that amateurs are capable of uplifting the dramatic stage, but it still remains to be demonstrated that amateurs are capable of uplifting the music show stage. A lot of amateurs have valiantly tried it, but up to date the extent of their improvement of the latter stage has not been such as to keep the MM. Ziegfeld and White awake at nights. In point of fact, the peaceful snores of the MM. Ziegfeld and White are still disturbingly audible. Once every few years some organization like the Neighborhood Playhouse puts on a revue that makes the gentlemen in question roll over a bit restlessly in their sleep, but it isn't long afterward that the rich and contentful snoring isn't going on as obstreperously as before.

The trouble with the amateurs who would show the MM. Ziegfeld and White how to do things is simple. They believe that the way to improve the revue stage is to improve on the "Follies" and "Scandals." Now, while the MM. Ziegfeld and White themselves would probably be the last men in the world to deny that the "Follies" and "Scandals" might be improved upon—the M. Ziegfeld has often admitted as much in the case of the "Scandals" and the M. White has just as often admitted as much in the case of the "Follies"—it is doubtful if this improvement may be effected by getting rid of W. C. Fields, Ann Pennington, George Gershwin, James Reynolds and Joseph Urban and substituting for them, respectively, a young man who is regarded as a hot comedian in the Greenwich Village cafeterias, an ex-tearoom manageress with bow-legs, a composer of melodies for violins made out of cigar boxes, a Macdougal Alley batik embroiderer and a second-hand pair of silk curtains. Yet that, in the main, is the way the amateurs go about it. They seem to imagine that the way to uplift the "Follies" and "Scandals" is to take out all the pretty girls, beautiful costumes, dazzling scenery, good tunes and funny comedians and put in their stead a few lyrics in imitation of W. S. Gilbert's, a scene in which they make sport of their own production's deficiencies and a program that cracks sarcastic jokes about every number on the bill. It doesn't work.

In order to improve the revue stage, something more is necessary than the amateurs seem to possess. One of the things is wit. Another is money. Somehow or other, it appears to be the amateurs' notion that the Charlot Revue, which most of them elect to imitate, was put on for about ten or twelve dollars. Just how this idea got around, it is difficult to make out. I assume that it got under way because Charlot showed no elaborate Ben Ali Haggin tableaux with elephants in them and no scene in which a hundred chorus girls marched down thirty golden steps and descended into a twenty-by-twenty-five foot trapdoor. But, alas, the Charlot Revue was anything but the shoestring investment it is supposed to have been. To put on any kind of revue with any degree of taste and loveliness takes money, and quite a bit of it. A revue written by George Bernard Shaw, Max Beerbohm, Ring Lardner, Franz Lehar and Oscar Strauss might be produced for less money than one written by the gentlemen currently entrusted with writing our revues, but unfortunately the amateurs haven't thus far succeeded in finding among their number any Shaw, Beerbohm, Lardner, Lehar or Strauss. These amateurs believe that if they have one fairly good sketch, one fairly good tune, a girl who can lift her right leg three feet in the air without falling over backward and a young man who can give an imitation of Beatrice Lillie, they are all set to drive Ziegfeld, White and Charlot out of business. But the best that they have been able to do thus far in that direction is to get some extravagantly laudatory notices from the newspaper reviewers and to boost Ziegfeld's, White's and Charlot's business proportionately.

§ 4

Nothing could be more provincial and absurd than the current demand that opera drop its born umlauts and accents and acquire, for the greater delectation of the Anglo-Saxon, an English speech. Opera in English is, in the main, just about as sensible a plea as baseball in Italian. The opera is not an Anglo-Saxon art form and to attempt arbitrarily, for patriotic reasons, to make it one is akin to Germanizing Georgian architecture or Frenchifying American jazz. The notion that you can get, say, French opera in English by the simple trick of translating, for example, "Les Huguenots" into English is like the notion that you can get American comedy in French by translating George Ade's "College Widow" into French and having the football team wear the Sorbonne colors. What results, obviously, is a hybrid, as unpersuasive and unconvincing as an Englishman talking American slang or a German wearing a monocle. The notion, further, that the way to get opera in English is to have the librettos written by English-speaking artists is a good notion so far as it goes, but an equally good notion is to have English-speaking artists first write music as good as Wagner's, Mozart's or even Papa Meyerbeer's.

§ 5

It is agreed without noticeable dissent that Chaliapin is the best singing actor on the modern operatic stage. It is further agreed that the operatic stage has known no such combination of dramatic talent and voice in its history. And it is also agreed that, aside from this rare combination of histrionic skill and vocal excellence, Chaliapin is as deficient a pantomimist as the same stage has known and a dancer approximately as graceful as an adult billy-goat. It is the aim and purpose of the Moscow Art Theatre Musical Studio, under the direction of the estimable Dantchenko, to turn out a troupe composed entirely of Chaliapins who are also expert in pantomime and virtuosi of Terpischore. It is similarly the aim and purpose of doctors of eugenics to turn out a troupe of men who shall be not only Chaliapins, but Hegels, Wellingtons, Sandows and Valentinos as well.

Dantchenko is to be commended for his intention and to be pitied for his faith. To convince one's self that his dream is impossible of achievement, all that one has to do is to view (1), the presentations he has been making in America in the last year and (2), the somewhat more general handiwork of the Lord God Almighty in the last nineteen hundred and twenty-six years. Dantchenko is a talented theatrical director, but God is against him. He can no more succeed in getting together a company of sixty men and women who are absolutely and equally perfect in acting, singing, dancing and pantomime, in all the dramatic, lyric and plastic possibilities of the stage, than Swedenborgians can complete the spirituality of *Homo sapiens* by training him in the "Arcana Cœlestia," showing him picture postcards of Emmanuel's magnificent whiskers and making him fix his mind on the Four Gospels instead of the Four Marx Brothers. The Russian regisseur's theory is at odds with nature. It is enough to expect of any human being, even, indeed, of any actor, that he be able to do one thing well. To hope for a Coquelin who can sing like a Caruso or for a De Reszké who can act like a Forbes-

Robertson, for a Duse who can dance like a Génee or an Irene Castle who can act like a Bernhardt, and that the unparagoned combination be, to boot, as proficient in pantomime as a Courtès or a Jane May, is to be a very major-general of optimists.

What Dantchenko has managed to get together is a troupe which can act considerably better than the average opera troupe and sing considerably worse. But the fellow is not without his sagacious wiles. At such junctures of his performances as the poor quality of a specific actor's singing must become obvious to his audience, he shrewdly distracts the latter's attention from the deficiency by a rapid and surprising reapportionment of those various parts of the song which are beyond the actor's capacity to such minor garlicos of his company as have been engaged for their ability to sing them and who, having done their bit, are then carefully allowed to fade politely from the scene. This is a trick that he works in his production of "Carmen," and it is a good trick. But it synchronously is one that betrays clearly the weakness of his whole scheme. Again, that scheme shows its clay foot in his production of Offenbach's "La Périchole." When this was disclosed initially in New York, Dantchenko entrusted the leading rôle to the best actress in his aggregation, Olga Baklanova. But it wasn't long before the director appreciated that an actress suited to the fiery dramatic interpretation of Carmen might not be so well suited to the milder dramatic interpretation of the rôle of the Spanish street-singer, and before a change was accordingly made in mid-stream, and, with the change, another smear of clay revealed in the whole Dantchenko so-called "synthetic theatre" plan. In the case of "Lysistrata," an exhibit in which hardly any singing and no dancing are called for, the Russians manage better, but "Lysistrata" is no more a test for a true synthetic theatre than "The Old Homestead."

Dantchenko's organization, in short, is excellent in the way of acting, pretty bad in the way of singing, and downright incompetent in the way of dancing. The Moscow Art Theatre, under Stanislavsky, achieved something approaching to perfection by confining its efforts to a single thing, to wit, dramatic acting. The Moscow Art Theatre Musical Studio, under Dantchenko, misses fire because it has spread its efforts over too wide a field. To obtain results in the theatre, a greater concentration is necessary.

§ 6

The decline of the audience is one of the saddest phenomena of modern American life. There

was a day, handily within memory, when the
American audience, whatever the spectacle it
figured before, was at least half the show, but
that day seems to have passed into melancholy
limbo. The audience, whether it be a baseball,
theatre, concert, opera, racetrack, circus or any
other kind of audience, is today approximately as
gay and animated as a three days' corpse. Not
only is it no longer part of the show; it actually
detracts from the show. Yet who doesn't remember the gay days when things were different,
when the audience was as lively as it now is life-
less? Those were the days when the baseball
bleachers were twice as diverting as the game itself, when the badinage was as of ten thousand
stewed George Ades and Finley Peter Dunnes in
action, when the hat stores for blocks around had
to keep open until after seven o'clock to refurbish
hundreds of heads, when pop bottles and cushions
were considered the height of repartee, when the
umpire was verbally murdered thousands of times
every afternoon, when volunteer low comedians
entertained the grand-stand as it has never been
entertained since. Those were the days when
theatre audiences made it necessary for Shakespearian hams to play behind nets, when an Ibsen
second act generally found the stage strewn with

dead tomatoes, when the hero of melodrama was warned that the villain was lying in ambush behind yon rock, when a hussy with a hole in her tights drew down thunders of applause, interrupted by considerable friendly advice, when the mere spectacle of an actor's false moustache becoming dislodged was sufficient to make ten or twelve willing pairs of hands crawl over the footlights to assist politely, if emphatically, in its readjustment. Those were the days when racetrack and football audiences, pickled to the eyebrows, contributed their mite to the *comédie humaine,* when opera audiences would cuckoo the performers' sour notes, when circus audiences fed lighted cigarettes to the elephants, stuck pins into the fat woman, and hung around after the show was over to beat up the actor who played Nero in the Kiralfy spectacles. Those days, alas, are no more. The American audiences have come to be so many blocks of wood. The youth, the spirit, the fun of America seem to have gone the way of all flesh.

§ 7

The average man amongst us who is assigned to the job of doing a Parisian farce over into English and of fitting it to the local stage generally

knows no more about the French spirit, manner
and idiosyncrasy than is to be gained from an
occasional brief Summer residence in a Paris flat
subleased from the Dolly Sisters or from a few
weeks' Springtime residence in a chair in front of
one of the Americanized boulevard cafés.   The result is that French farce as we usually get it from
our adaptors is accurate enough in the way of substituting the right English word for the French one,
but otherwise no more internally suggestive of the
French spirit than "Die Wacht am Rhein."

§ 8

If the manager of the Giants were to schedule
a baseball game and officially open the season in
the third week of December, one would be forgiven for hinting that the fellow was not entirely
intact in the region north of his horn spectacles.
But when a theatrical manager blandly schedules
a play and officially opens the season in the third
week of July, anyone who would so much as suggest that he was *non compos* would immediately
have a $100,000 libel suit on his hands.   Just
how any good business man—of which there are
rumored to be one or two among our fifty or sixty
producing managers—persuades himself that the
time to begin putting on plays is when July is

hottest, when all the more intelligent ushers and stagehands are still at their country places and when the only people in town are the kind who go to the theatre only when they get in free, is not easy to deduce. Yet year in and year out we find such presumably good business men doing that very thing. Where one of these men wouldn't think for a moment of buying Mexican oil stocks, Arizona real estate, mortgages on suburban Shakespearian theatres or any other such goldbricks, he apparently doesn't hesitate for an instant to put his money into the worst theatrical month of the year. And when his play subsequently fails to bring stampedes of New Yorkers to the box-office, he lodges the blame upon the reviewers, the actor who tripped over a chair on the opening night and forgot one of his lines, the failure of his press-agent to get a picture of the leading woman on the first page of the Sunday *Times*' theatrical section, the circumstance that Morris Gest impolitely left after the first act and so prejudiced all the critics against the show, and the too strong competition of the "Follies" and the Winter Garden revue. In short, upon everything but the fact that on hot July nights the average man no more cares to sit in a dramatic theatre than the average hoochie-coochie dancer cares to sit on a cake of ice.

§ 9

The ideas of nine out of every ten present-day
London stage producers in the matter of scenic
investiture go back to the days when furniture was
painted on the backdrop and when a "big production" was any one in which the stage was so
packed and crowded with scenery and irrelevant
but costly props that the actors had to make their
entrances from the wings sidewise. Their ideas
of lighting, further, are based upon the theory
that all that is necessary to achieve some exceptionally beautiful illumination effects are a half
dozen vari-colored gelatine slides supplemented
by an indefatigable fellow stationed at the dim-
mer. And their ideas of dramatic pace are similarly reminiscent of that epoch in the theatre when
scene and act intermissions were arbitrarily regu-
lated by the time it took the candy butchers in the
aisles to dispose of a sufficient number of prize
packages.

§ 10

The present-day circus is much less a circus
than a vaudeville show with a smell. Every other
act is a Keith-Orpheum act, and with little more

relation to a good old-fashioned circus than a straight three-card-monte game. There, in the good old rings where once the evil Bruno, man-eating lion from the African wild, snarled and snapped at the handsome Prof. Albert Delatour, the world's most debonair animal trainer, we have now Alf Loyal's trained dog act from the Palace Theatre. There, in the circle of sawdust, where once Comanche Joe lassooed Big Nose Blower, the Indian chief, we see now Lillian Leitzel, late of the Orpheum Circuit and the Ziegfeld "Frolic," and Mijares, out of a Shubert Winter Garden show. And there, in those rings of our youth where once Algernon, the trick bear, danced a waltz with the chubby and bespangled Mlle. Aleta, we have now May Wirth, of the Hippodrome, and the Hanne-fords, from the same playhouse. In place of the exciting old chariot race, there are a series of liv-ing pictures like those in the old Hanlon extrava-ganzas and in place of the sweet one who was shot from the mouth of a cannon, there are tango dan-cers and a Cinderella pageant. If this constitutes a circus, as all of us youngsters know a circus, then pink lemonade is made by Schlitz. Gone forever is the show that boasted a calliope, popcorn in bags greasy with warm butter instead of in machine-made round molasses-covered cakes, the shell game

277

and the act in which La Belle Juanita Fernandez
was strapped to the back of a white horse and was
chased around the ring by twenty Irishmen dressed
as Arabs. The present circus has not one ring,
or two rings, or three rings, or four rings—but five
rings. Yet five rings do not necessarily make a
circus any more than five rings make a duchess.

§ 11

The so-called little theatres which presently dot
the country, being about the size of the average
steamer trunk, are so intimate that if you whisper to a girl sitting next to you in the last row
that you'd like to take her to supper a girl sitting
in the first row answers yes. The ushers are able
to show persons to their seats from the rear aisle
simply by pointing. And the audience is so close
to itself that if one member of it sneezes all the
others believe that it is themselves and wipe their
noses. Plainly enough, it is not easy for a play
to establish what is known as the theatre mood in
such a theatre. The feel of the theatre is lacking.
Sitting in such a playhouse, one feels the theatre-
pull little more than one feels it in a street-car.
And it is an unusual play that is able to triumph
over the deficiency.

278

§ 12

As a general rule, the more pretentious the name of a company or organization is, the surer you are to have to walk up six flights of stairs and stumble over eight or ten soap boxes and a lot of empty beer bottles to find it. Anything called simply the Standard Oil Company you'll find on the ground floor, but when you run across something elegantly named the Ultra-Imperial and Non-Pareil Transcontinental and Mid-Rumanian Novelty Company, you are safe in putting up your last nickel that it is situated in a two-by-four office next to the rear fire escape on the eleventh floor of a shaky frame building in the vicinity of the gas works. It is the same way in the theatre. The simple Arthur Hopkinses and Theatre Guilds may usually be relied upon to produce the plays worth seeing, and the fancily dubbed corporations to produce the kind of plays that boost business considerably in the nearby speakeasies.

§ 13

It seems to be the general opinion at present that all it takes to be a theatrical producer is a friend in Wall Street, some printed stationery, a press-agent, and a box of Corona Corona cigars. There was a time when things were different and when it was required of a producer that he at least have some years of experience and training, to say nothing of a charge account in the lunch room at the Hotel Astor. But those days, like many others, are past. Today any man who has a play manuscript, a bowing acquaintance with the dramatic critic of the *Bronx Home News* and three props consisting of a telephone, a revolver and a clock that strikes twelve considers himself all fixed to enter into competition with Belasco, Ames, Erlanger and the Shuberts. Among the suddenly constituted producers who have entered the theatre in the last two years, there have been two former automobile salesmen, four recently discharged office-boys, one sandwich-restaurant owner, one baker, seven one-night-stand actors, five curb brokers, one coal dealer, three former icemen, two ex-firemen, four silk merchants, six cloak and suit dealers, eight dramatic critics, one chiropractor, three ward politicians, one clarinet player, two lime and cement dealers, five toilet preparation manufacturers, and one designer of ladies' underdrawers. All but three of these producers may at the present time be addressed in care of the poorhouse. Two of the others are in sanitoriums, and the third is about to invest the $3,000 net profit he made on his first production in a play dealing with a crook who reforms in the last act.

§ 14

How much longer, I wonder, are we to view producers idiotic enough to believe that they can work up a modern audience to a thrill of excitement with the villain-heroine game of sexual tag? For thirty-five years now theatre audiences have squatted patiently in their chairs watching libidinous dark gentlemen gallumph around rooms after chaste and yelling ingénues, only to be baffled by heart failure, a sudden attack of morals, a paper-knife, or the entrance of Lucien, the waiter, or of young Basil Balderdash, the girl's fiancé and the *Daily Mail's* star reporter. For years these audiences have prayed, fasted, burned candles, contributed money to the missionaries and crossed the palms of gipsies in the hope that they might at least once see the villain recompense them for the price they paid out for their seats, but to no avail. The result is that today such business simply makes an audience snicker. You can fool it no longer. It has been a sucker too often.

§ 15

At the present time, five theatres are running full-blast on the Bowery. They embrace two Chinese and two Yiddish theatres and one Italian theatre. I went down the other night and had a look at them.

The leading difference between these Yiddish theatres and the Broadway theatres is that one generally finds more Jews in the Broadway theatres. The Chinese theatres, on the other hand, are chiefly remarkable for the amount of peanuts the Chinamen in the audience eat during the show. The manager of one of the theatres informed me that, on the average, an audience of seven hundred Chinamen eats seven thousand bags of peanuts from eight o'clock to eleven. What is more, the Chinaman, I observed, appears to enjoy a peanut principally because of the noise it makes. A theatre full of Chinamen eating peanuts sounds like a Wild West show. The Chinaman has a technic all his own for cracking the shells. The mere Anglo-Saxon, unversed in the culture of the East, simply cracks the peanut shell between his thumb and forefinger and lets it go at that. But not the Chinaman. The Chinaman isn't content amateurishly to crack the peanut shell once; he must crack it four times—with his fingers first, then with his teeth, then with his shoe, and finally by sitting on it and bouncing up and down. A theatre full of Chinamen eating peanuts is thus indistinguishable from a Robert B. Mantell performance of "King Lear."

The Italian theatre is not so highly perfumed as the Yiddish and not so noisy as the Chinese, but it, too, has its individuality. The individuality of the Italian theatre consists in its audience's enthusiasm. Where the Chinaman wouldn't condescend to move so much as a muscle even if the villain of a play bit the heroine in two, and where the Yiddisher considers his money well spent if he is vouchsafed merely a couple of good cries, the Italian comports himself in the theatre something like a cross between a thunderstorm and an earthquake. He responds to every stage emotion like an engine going to a four-alarm fire. If the heroine's stern father drives her out into the cold, our friend, the wop, bawls as no child has ever bawled for Castoria, and if the hero neatly baffles the villain, our friend's joy is akin to that of a doctor during a smallpox epidemic.

On the night I explored the Bowery, one of the Chinese theatres was showing a Chinese drama and the other a Chinese opera. I decided to see the former first. After an half hour's stay in the theatre, I bethought me the opera might be more to

my taste, and I made to take my departure. On
reaching the door, the manager was solicitous as
to the reason for my leaving.

"I wish to go down to the other Chinese theatre
and see the opera," I said.

He gave me a pained look. "But this *is* the
opera!" he exclaimed.

It appears that a Chinese opera consists of a
character who sits at stage centre and recites what
seems to be the Chinese equivalent of "Curfew
Shall Not Ring To-night," while three Chinese
gents in shirt-sleeves sit at stage right and pound,
respectively, on a board, a lead pipe and an empty
Campbell's soup can.

So I went to one of the Yiddish theatres.

The play of the evening, I was told by an attendant stationed on the sidewalk, was a Yiddish
classic known as "His Mother's Son" or "His
Son's Mother"; the attendant didn't seem to be
sure which. When I came out of the theatre at
the end of the act, I asked him again. He told me
it was "Her Daughter's Father." Just what the
exhibit, whatever it was, was about, I fear that I
shall be unable to tell you. So far as I could make
out from what I saw of it, it seemed to concern
an aristocratic old Hebrew family, the son of which
promenaded the costly drawing-room elegantly

outfitted in plus-fours and made love to a young woman dressed as a Red Cross nurse without the cross. Just before the curtain fell on the act, an old man tottered into the drawing-room and gave the son a loud box on the ear, whereupon the girl dressed as a nurse fainted. I assume that the play was a sad one, as considerable sniffling on the part of the audience reached my ears.

At the Italian theatre, my next stop, a popular melodrama was going on. The popular Italian melodramas are all very much alike. When the hero isn't busy getting down on his knees and praying to the Redeemer to grant his wish and save the heroine's life, the heroine is busy getting down on hers and praying to the Redeemer to save her baby's life. Mix up these prayers with a scene in which some one is choked, a scene in which some one is struck across the cheek with the blade of a stiletto and a scene in which the villagers rush in and find the innocent hero bending suspiciously over the corpse, and you have the kind of show that the Italian yokel regards with an eminent favor.

The average Italian melodrama seldom fails to disclose three rubber-stamp lines. No. 1 is "You must trust in God, for He alone knows all our sorrows." No. 2 is "Mary—she was a mother! So perhaps she can understand another mother's woes!" And No. 3 is "My child—he moves; he speaks; he lives! The Lord be praised!"

The Chinese theatre where the Chinese drama was on view next drew my attention. The only thing about the drama that I could understand was the pretty Chinese girl who played what I guess was the rôle of the heroine.

When I came out of the theatre, I asked the manager, who was standing in the lobby, what the play was about.

"How the hell should I know?" was his indignant reply.

§ 16

An encouraging sign of improvement in the quality of the American theatrical audience is the failure of the propaganda play any longer to make the impression it once did. Up to within a few years, the propaganda play was prosperous at the box-office. All that a playwright had to do to fetch in audiences was to convert "Camille" into a slum drama pleading for safeguards against the spread of tuberculosis or dress up the leading character in "What Happened To Jones" to look like Jesus Christ and present the result as a plea for the brotherhood of man and a consequent raise

286

in wages for the West Virginia coal miners. Those were the tulip days when theatres were crowded with imbeciles sitting open-mouthed before melodramatic trash made to seem important by incorporating into it a couple of admonitory speeches on the social diseases and revampings of such German dramas as Max Dreyer's "Pastor's Daughter of Streladorf" into which some crafty Broadway showmaker had stuck a ten minute address on equal sex rights for women. Those were the days when one couldn't go into a theatre without hearing a considerable indignation over Tammany Hall, the corruption of juries, the stigma that clung to the woman with a past, capital punishment and what not. Times, however, appear to have changed for the better. No longer do our audiences take indignation with them into a theatre, although, one must confess, they often enough take it out of a theatre with them. No longer are our audiences profoundly moved by soap-box lectures, Bible tracts and patent medicine circulars in the form of drama.

§ 17

Every merchant of words is more or less a Peter Whiffle. Though he confect a hundred books, there are always a hundred more that he

287

at one time or another has planned to write but that he never has written and never will write. Thus, though I have thought about doing it for years, I know that I shall never write a book on the American sideshow. Yet to me there is no more beckoning subject, for the circus, carnival and street-fair sideshow has in it, as I see it, a wealth of material for the delectation of all epicures of the rich and juicy in American buncombe.

The sideshow is, in certain of its manifestations, a typical American institution, as native as Sitting Bull, Cal Coolidge and reversible undershirts. It is no more like the French sideshows that periodically embellish the *foires* in the Boulevard de Clichy or the German sideshows that one encounters on Charlottenburg sand-lots on the equivalent of American circus days or the English sideshows of, say, Wembley, than the Boston Symphony Orchestra is like the Swiss Bell Ringers. It isn't that the performers are always different from those in the other sideshows; as a matter of fact, at least one-third of the performers are importations; it is that, in the manner of presentation, in the way of elaboration, in the ingenuity of its unearthing of bogus phenomena and in its bulk and size it differs from the transmarine sideshow as

288